THE
COFFEE AND TEA
COOKBOOK

Christie and Thomas Katona

Bristol Publishing Enterprises
Hayward, California

CONTENTS

THE HISTORY OF COFFEE

By most accounts the discovery of coffee took place around 600 A.D. It is widely believed that Ethiopian tribesmen discovered the coffee plant growing wild while tending their herds. The tribesmen mixed the ground berries with animal fat and rolled the resulting mixture into balls for eating during their journeys. For the next 400 years the berries were used primarily for food (although some resourceful person discovered the berries could be fermented into wine). The use and cultivation of coffee beans eventually migrated to Arabia, where somewhere between the 10th and 15th centuries, the Arabs learned to steep the beans in water to make a delicious brew they called "qahwa." The brew, considered by some to be a potent medicine, was known for its restorative powers as well as being a delicious beverage. By the end of the 15th century Arabian coffee houses were popular meeting places, and coffee was a part of Arabian life.

As early as the 13th century, coffee was shipping from Arabian ports including Mocha, which gives this famous coffee bean its name. The enterprising Arabian merchants who grew and sold the beans shrewdly prevented any viable seeds and coffee plants from being exported, to protect their monopoly on the product. For several hundred years they successfully kept the source of the beans to themselves and enjoyed a brisk trade and high profits.

In the 17th century a Moslem pilgrim successfully smuggled a plant or seeds home to his native India. From this humble start, the first coffee plantation in India was started at Karnatak and quickly spread to dozens of countries. Dutch traders purchased some of the trees from the Karnatak plantation and began cultivating them in Java, which is the source of the Mocha Java blend.

A young French naval officer, Captain Gabriel Mathieu de Clieu, is credited with bringing the plant to the Caribbean via Martinique, where it spread throughout the West Indies and eventually to Central and South America. The single plant he brought to Martinique appears to be the progenitor of most of the billions of coffee plants which are now the major source of the world's coffee. The plant acquired (stolen) by De Clieu was a descendent of a coffee plant given as a gift to Louis XIV. The king's coffee plants were cultivated in a hothouse at Louie XIV's Jardin des Plantes and were kept under close guard. De Clieu was able to obtain one of the plants through a romantic liaison with a lady of the court who had access to the hothouse; the rest is history.

Romance also played a part in the spread of coffee production to Brazil. There is evidence that Brazil clandestinely acquired the plant through Dutch Guiana, where a Brazilian Army Lieutenant smuggled the plant back to Brazil with the aid of the wife of the local governor who was enamored with the Lieutenant.

Coffee use spread from Arabia first to Turkey and eventually to Europe. It appears that Venetian traders were responsible for introducing coffee to European markets. The first coffee house in England opened in 1637 and within three decades had spread throughout the country. English coffeehouses became a center for social, intellectual, commercial and political discussions. These coffee houses became known as "penny universities" because by paying a penny admission price, you could hear intellectual discussions as well as the latest gossip and news while enjoying your cup of coffee.

In the American colonies, the Dutch had introduced English style coffee-houses, but until the American revolution and the Boston Tea Party, tea was the preferred American beverage. Starting with the boycott of English tea, the beverage of choice in America became coffee and to date has remained the preferred beverage for most Americans.

COFFEE PRODUCTION

While there are many species of coffee trees in the world, only two have any economic significance, coffea arabica and coffea canephora, or as they are more commonly known, arabica and robusta coffees. Although both species originated in the same general region between Africa and Asia, they are now grown in numerous countries in a band stretching about 25 degrees north and south of the equator. The arabica beans are the higher quality "gourmet" beans while the robusta beans are less expensive and the primary bean used in the canned and instant coffee found in your local neighborhood grocery store.

The arabica coffee trees thrive at higher altitudes, generally between 5,000 and 8,000 feet. In these higher altitudes the beans mature at a slower pace, which gives them time to produce a richer, denser, more flavorful bean known in the trade as a "hard bean."

On the other hand, the robusta coffee trees grown at lower altitudes have many advantages for the producer. They are easier to cultivate, more disease-resistant, can tolerate larger temperature and moisture extremes, produce more beans, and their fruit matures considerably quicker than their arabica counterparts. They also have about twice as much caffeine which partly accounts for their harsher taste. The net result is a bean which is cheaper to produce, albeit less flavorful.

The coffee tree is an evergreen which grows to about fifteen feet high and ten feet across; however, on farms and plantations the trees are typically trimmed to no more than eight or nine feet high and about six feet across to facilitate harvesting. Coffee trees start to produce blossoms at three to fours years of age and are fully mature at about seven years. The coffee tree's blossoms are creamy white, with a sweet-smelling fragrance resembling orange blossoms or jasmine. The blossoms eventually close and develop into small sweet berries somewhat like elongated cranberries which are at first green, then ripen into bright crimson fruit called cherries. The arabica tree cherries ripen in about six to nine months while robusta trees take only about three months to mature, mostly due to their lower growing elevation.

The coffee beans you grind at home are the seeds of these coffee cherries. Within the pulp of each cherry are two flat-sided seeds. Each seed has a thin, tight-fitting inner skin called the "silverskin" and a yellowish outer husk called the "parchment". A healthy coffee tree produces about 2000 beans per year.

Coffee cherries are processed by either the wet or dry method. The dry method is the oldest and cheapest and is used primarily where water is in short supply or where wet processing equipment is not available. It consists of drying the fruit on the tree or shaking or stripping the fruit from the tree and then sun-drying it on cement or packed-earth patios. Generally this method results in inferior coffee because the underripe and overripe berries are processed along with the good beans. After the cherries are dried they are packed in bags and transported to mills in large cities where machines are used to remove the dried cherry pulp, the silverskin and the parchment. The beans are then sorted and graded according to the methods of the country and of the local producer.

The wet method consists of feeding freshly picked cherries through machines which separate the seeds from the pulp. As the mixture is fed through water, the lighter pulp floats to the top and is removed, leaving the seeds behind. The seeds are put into liquid-filled storage tanks for 24 to 48 hours and allowed to ferment slightly to remove an outer mucilage coating before final washing and drying.

After the fermentation process, the seeds are dried to about a 10 percent moisture content. The drying is usually done on cement patios but more recently is done with tumbling dryers which greatly speed up the process. During the drying process the seeds shrink within their silverskin and parchment coverings. At this point, the dried covering and the beans themselves are referred to as "pergamino". These pergamino beans can be stored for a considerable period without a significant effect on their flavor. The next stage of processing is to put the pergamino beans through hulling or milling machines which gently remove the silverskin and parchment coverings and give the beans a polished look. The longer the beans are milled, the more polished and attractive they appear. However, it is also possible to damage the beans if they are overmilled or exposed to too much heat. Heat produced from too much friction can remove the natural wax coating on the surface of each bean which seals in the volatile aromatic flavors. If over-processed, the complexity and quality of the final cup of coffee will be diminished.

CHOOSING COFFEE

WHERE TO BUY IT

While gourmet coffee was once the province of esoteric specialty shops, it is now available in large variety at most of the jumbo supermarkets. However, the specialty shops still have a much broader selection of coffee as well as coffee makers and accessories. We prefer the specialty shops just for the atmosphere, but you will also find they have both a broader knowledge of the product and a shared enthusiasm for the product that you just won't find in any supermarket. We still find it a wonderful experience to walk into a specialty store and find ourselves assaulted by an array of heady coffee aromas.

KNOWING YOUR BEANS

Although quality coffees are made from arabica beans, you may still be bewildered by the variety of arabica coffees available at your local coffee store. These stores offer a large selection of pure, unblended coffees usually distinguished by country of origin or perhaps by the major port from which they are exported. Coffee names such as Cinnamon, Full City, or French are used to distinguish coffees by the amount of roasting they have received.

Pure beans from each country and regions have unique flavor characteristics that are determined by their native climate and soil conditions. Retailers blend these pure coffees in an attempt to combine the best flavor characteristics of each country.

How the beans are roasted is very important to the final flavor of your coffee. There are three roasting stages that the beans pass through as they progress from green beans to the rich brown coffee beans we find at the store. In the first stage, the beans are heated to bring the water in the beans close to the boiling point which drives off all free moisture in the beans. In the second stage, heat, air flow and roasting time are carefully controlled by the roastmaster to bring the internal temperature of the beans to between 320° and 480°, depending on the bean type and roast desired. During this stage, the natural sugars of the bean caramelize, which results in the characteristically rich brown color of the roasted beans. This breakdown process, called pyrolosis, produces new substances not found in the original green bean. New aromatic substances are formed, along with oils, fats, waxes and carbohydrates which add to the flavor complexity in the final brewed cup of coffee. The oils, fats, and carbohydrates provide body and help suspend and contain the many delicate and volatile aromatics within the cup.

As the roast continues, additional complex substances are broken down into simpler components and the many volatile oils are driven outward toward the bean's surface. This is considered the third stage and is characterized by an oily appearance on the outside of the bean. "Full city roast" is a term used to describe this approximate stage. It is the darkest roast achievable before the volatile oils are driven off by further application of heat. Going beyond this point such as for "French" or "Italian" "roasts" drives some of the aromatics completely from the beans, as well as some of the unique and distinguishing flavors. For these types of roasts, the roastmaster chooses to trade off those distinguishing varietal flavors in favor of the French roast taste that some people prefer. Luckily, the retail houses provide us with a tremendous variety of beans and roasts from which to choose.

The following terminology is in common use within the coffee industry. However, the terminology may vary somewhat by locale. For example French roast is a commonly used term for both the darker and darkest roast as shown below.

Light Roasts
Light
Pale
Cinnamon
Half City

Darker Roasts
Dark
Continental
Vienna or Viennese
New Orleans
French

Medium Roasts
Medium
Regular
Full City
American

Darkest Roasts
French
Italian
Espresso

TASTING

Ultimately, tasting is the most important method of judging coffee quality. A few basic terms should be in your repertoire. The three fundamental tasting terms you should be familiar with are flavor, body and acidity.

Flavor is the overall impression of aroma, body and acidity. It generally has two connotations. First, it can be used to describe taste in a general sense like "rich and mellow" or "bitter and harsh." Second, it can be used in a comparative sense, in which the brew might be described as tasting like nuts or a particular spice such as cinnamon, or for some less-than-perfect beans, like burnt rubber.

Body describes the tactile impression of the weight and texture of the coffee within the mouth. Terms used to describe it range from "thin and watery" at one extreme to "buttery" and even "syrupy" at the other extreme. The sensation of oiliness within the mouth is a measure of the fat content, and the overall sensation of viscosity is a measure of the protein, carbohydrate and fiber content of the cup.

Acidity describes how lively the cup is as opposed to being dull and flat tasting. It has nothing to do with how much acid it contains (pH factor). High acidity is one of the distinguishing characteristics of high grown arabicas and is considered a positive characteristic. Words used to further describe coffee acidity are those like crisp, sharp, keen, pungent or tangy. Another way to describe the acidity of a cup is in terms of how much "snap" it has. If a cup is described as having a lot of snap, it has a high acidity.

ESPRESSO

Most people associate the term "espresso" with a concentrated and bitter brew. But espresso, properly made, makes an extremely flavorful cup since it is brewed rapidly and served immediately while at peak freshness. The term espresso is Italian for fast. The espresso method uses pressure rather than gravity to rapidly extract the essence of the coffee in a concentrated form. Espresso is also used to describe the blend of beans and the degree of roast for the beans used to prepare espresso. Espresso roast is one of the darkest roasts and is characterized by a slightly burnt flavor.

If you want to prepare your own espresso there are many espresso machines available in specialty stores intended for home use, ranging from less expensive "Moka "pots which are heated on your burner, to very sophisticated espresso machines. Gaggia, Krups, Pavoni, Bellina, Benjamin and Medwin, and Avanti are some of the better known brand names. Some machines also have a cappuccino nozzle that uses the steam generated by the machine to steam and froth milk.

All of the machines work by forcing hot, pressurized water through finely ground espresso coffee that is tamped into a filter basket to make individual cups of espresso. Since pressure is used to extract the coffee essence, the variables of grind, quantity, tamp and rate of pour have a greater influence on the final taste than they do in the regular drip process for normal coffee.

The right amount of espresso coffee is determined by the capacity of your machine. Generally, you will fill your filter insert almost completely, leaving just a little room for expansion of the grounds. Most home machines use about $1\frac{1}{2}$ tbs. per cup. The rate of pour is best determined by experiment. As a guideline your machine should produce about 1 to $1\frac{1}{4}$ ounces of espresso in about 25 seconds for a single shot machine.

You will find that there is an enormous variety of espresso-based drinks as well as flavored steamed milk drinks available at espresso bars. Below is a list of the basics you should find at any modern espresso stand:

Espresso Macchiato	An espresso "marked" with a dollop of milk foam.
Espresso con Panna	An espresso topped with a dollop of whipped cream.
Espresso Ristretto	A short pour (less than 1 ounce) which is accomplished by turning the pump off a few seconds earlier than normal.
Latte Macchiato	A cup of steamed milk "marked" with a shot of espresso. Steamed milk is added first, then topped with foam, and the espresso is added last by pouring it through the foam which leaves the mark.
Caffe Latte	A shot of espresso added to steamed or foamed milk.
Caffe Mocha	Espresso mixed with steamed milk and chocolate syrup.
Cappuccino	This drink contains approximately $1/3$ espresso, $1/3$ hot steamed milk, and $1/3$ foamed milk. Its name comes from the foamy cap on the drink, resembling the white hooded robes worn by Capuchin friars.
Breve	A latte made with steamed half-and-half.
Steamer	Steamed milk with a flavored syrup. Almond, vanilla, and hazelnut are popular; however, there are flavors available that range from interesting to bizarre.

FLAVORED COFFEES

Flavored coffees have been around since the first coffee infusions were prepared in the Middle East. These early coffee drinkers included spices such as cinnamon, nutmeg, cardamom, pepper and nuts in their coffee.

Commercial flavored coffees are now made by spraying liquid or powdered flavorings over hot roasted beans and then quickly drying and packaging them. Coffee houses use both natural and artificial flavorings. Those houses which use only natural flavorings insist they are better since they are more subtle and do not leave an artificial aftertaste in the mouth.

Flavored coffees generally have a more intense smell than taste due to the aromatic nature of the flavorings. Because aromatics have low boiling points by nature, their aromas are released continually along with the steam in the cup. The delicious smells imparted are savored as much as the taste by many consumers as witnessed by the fact that flavored coffees are now the fastest growing specialty market for coffee retailers.

The large supermarkets are cashing in on this trend and do a thriving business in flavored coffees. Some of the more popular flavored coffees are Irish cream, chocolate, vanilla, Swiss mocha, amaretto and macadamia nut.

DECAFFEINATED COFFEES

The stimulating effect of caffeine on the nervous system is well known and the increased alertness it provides is considered a desirable side benefit to many drinkers. However, the effects of caffeine are also a serious concern to many health-conscious people.

Caffeine is a mild central nervous system stimulant that in moderate amounts poses no health problems to most individuals. But it is also known that excessive consumption can cause sleeplessness and irritate the stomach. The tolerance to caffeine varies so widely among individuals that you will have to be your own judge regarding the amount you can consume in a day without negative side effects.

An average cup of caffeinated coffee contains 100 to 150 milligrams of caffeine, whereas a cup of decaf contains 2 to 5 milligrams. Use these figures as guidelines but remember that actual caffeine content varies greatly depending on the coffee. Remember also that coffee may not be the only source of caffeine in your diet. Tea, chocolate, soft drinks like Coca-Cola, and some over-the-counter drugs all contain varying amounts of caffeine.

There is also some concern about whether removing caffeine affects flavor and whether the process itself poses any health risk by leaving behind residual chemicals in the beans. Caffeine by itself is tasteless and odorless and its presence or absence has little or no effect on the flavor of the coffee. However, because all decaffeinating processes affect the chemical structure of the beans in varying degrees, they can and do affect the flavor in a negative way. The degree to which beans are affected depends on the process used.

MAKING GOOD COFFEE

Regardless of the brewing equipment you choose to use, there are a few essentials to making good coffee at home:

1. Start with good quality beans.
2. Use clean equipment.
3. Use fresh water.
4. Use the correct grind for your equipment.
5. Use the right amount of coffee.
6. Use the right water temperature for brewing.
7. Serve coffee fresh.

The importance of good quality coffee beans is paramount. If you start with inferior beans, you can't expect to brew a great cup of coffee. Clean equipment is important as well. Remember that coffee contains oils and other substances that get deposited on your equipment. If not removed, these residual substances deteriorate when exposed to air and will taint subsequent batches of coffee. When cleaning those portions of the equipment that come in contact with the brew, avoid using dish soap since a small amount tends to remain and will add an unwanted flavor to your next pot. Instead, use a non-abrasive scrubber with a little baking soda and then rinse thoroughly with fresh water.

If you're lucky to have a clean, fresh-tasting water supply in your city, then cool running tap water will make a great cup of coffee. If your water has enough minerals or other substances to color the taste, then consider a water filter or bottled spring water. If using tap water, let the cold water run for a time to aerate the water. Remember that your final coffee is still about 98 percent water.

The amount of coffee you should use for a full-bodied and flavorful cup of coffee is 2 level tablespoons per 6-ounce cup. People who try to skimp on the quantity of coffee or who grind coffee extra fine in an attempt to squeeze the maximum amount out of the grounds just end up with thin, bitter coffee. If you go to all the trouble to buy quality beans and properly handle them to retain their flavor, don't ruin your coffee at this final stage of preparation by trying to stretch it.

Most experts believe the best brewing temperature for coffee is between 195°F and 205°F. This temperature provides the best extraction of the coffee essence from the beans. Automatic drip machines designed for home use have their thermostats set in this range but remember to use cold water to ensure consistency in the brewing time.

Finally, serve the coffee fresh. The flavorful aromatics in fresh brewed coffee start to evaporate immediately after brewing and there is a noticeable loss of flavor after about 20 minutes if left on the hot plate. Probably the best and easiest course of action is to pour the freshly brewed coffee into a vacuum thermos bottle where it will retain its freshness far longer than sitting out in the open.

COFFEE BREWERS

There are a wide variety of coffee brewers on the market. By far the most popular home units are the automatic drip coffee makers because of their ease of use and the fact that they are priced in a range most people can afford. They make a pretty good cup of coffee, especially since additional accessories like metal mesh filters have become widely available.

Espresso machines are fairly popular, but the higher cost and extra skill required to make a good cup have kept some buyers at bay.

Percolators, with which the over-thirty crowd grew up, are still around but are not recommended for good coffee. They recirculate the brewed coffee from the bottom of the pot to the top to drench the coffee grounds over and over. This boiling of the coffee and over-extraction of the grounds tends to make the coffee bitter.

A French press is a type of plunger pot which produces a cup with a lot of body. After coffee grounds are added to the container, hot water is poured over them and the mixture is allowed to steep for a period. Then a plunger is used to force the grounds to the bottom of the container, leaving the brewed coffee above. Because a mesh screen is used instead of paper filters, the resulting coffee has more suspended oils and other substances to remain in the brew, which some people prefer. This type of brewer is a little harder to clean up and since the grounds remain somewhat in contact with the liquid, the brew tends to take on a strong taste after awhile.

There are a number of other interesting brewers you will find in your specialty store like vacuum pots, cold water extractors, Italian Neapolitan flips and other stove-top units, and Turkish ibriks, all of which can make good coffee.

STORING COFFEE AT HOME

Coffee, by its nature, is such that its many complex flavors are just at their peak as they leave the roaster. Unfortunately, coffee's wonderful flavor and aroma also begin to deteriorate immediately after roasting if left exposed to air. Exposure to air causes the oils responsible for coffee's flavor and aroma to evaporate. Unless protected in some manner, whole beans have only about a two-week life before their freshness and peak flavors disappear. The flavor and aroma of ground coffee will deteriorate within hours since it has much more surface area exposed to the air.

The best advice is to keep whole beans in an airtight container until ready to use and then grind only the amount you need to use. If you need to store coffee beans for longer lengths of time (up to three months), the best method is to place the beans in airtight containers and freeze them. You may want to store the beans in several small containers in the freezer because returning thawed unused beans to the freezer will result in moisture condensation which also causes flavor loss.

COFFEE DRINKS

THE EVER POPULAR LATTE

A good latte consists of a freshly drawn shot of espresso combined with steamed milk, heated to between 150° and 170°F and then topped by ¼ inch of foamed milk. Many syrups and toppings can be added to the latte. We find that fruit flavors go better with cold coffee and are delightful in the summer when added to Italian sodas. Fruit syrups are very good added to steamed milk, when they are called a "steamer." The most popular brands of syrups include Stasero, Torani and Davinci. Listed here are some of the flavors.

LATTE FLAVORS

almond
amaretto
banana
boysenberry
cherry
chocolate
cinnamon
coconut
crème de cacao
crème de menthe

hazelnut
Irish cream
kiwi
lemon
lime
orange
passion fruit
peach
raspberry
vanilla

TOPPINGS AND ADDITIONS

cinnamon

cocoa powder

honey

nutmeg

sugar

vanilla powder

VARIATIONS AND COMBINATIONS

Here are some interesting coffee drinks and combinations to get you started.

What's the Use?	-latte made with decaf coffee and skim milk
Mocha Lite	-mocha latte made with sugar-free cocoa
Chocolatino	-mocha latte made with Mexican chocolate
Mud Slide	-double shot of espresso with chocolate, topped with whipped cream
Mocha Moo	-mocha latte with almond
Mocha Mint	-mocha latte with mint syrup
Almond Joy	-mocha latte with almond and coconut syrup
Mounds	-mocha latte with coconut syrup
Milky Way	-mocha latte with caramel ice cream topping stirred in
Egg Nog Latte	-latte made with steamed egg nog
Apple Pie	-latte with apple and cinnamon syrup
Irish Cream	-latte made with Irish Cream syrup and half-and-half

AFTER-DINNER COFFEES

The combination of good after-dinner coffee with a touch of liqueur and topped with whipped cream is hard to beat. Besides the usual Irish coffee, try making one of these delicious combinations. If you wish a sweeter drink, add brown sugar to the coffee or sweeten the whipped cream.

BASIC RECIPE FOR ONE SERVING

6 oz. freshly brewed hot coffee
liqueur of your choice

whipped cream

Pour coffee into a cup, stir in liqueur and top with whipped cream.

MOCHA
   1 oz. Kahlua
   1 oz. crème de cacao

KAUAI NIGHTCAP
   1 oz. Tuaca
   1 oz. Grand Marnier

KOLOA COFFEE
   1 oz. brandy
   1 oz. macadamia nut liqueur

KONA NUT
   1 oz. Kahlua
   1 oz. Frangelico

BROWN VELVET
    1 oz. Triple Sec
    1 oz. crème de cacao

MINT PATTY
    1 oz. crème de menthe
    1 oz. cream de cacao

SPANISH EYES
    1 oz. Kahlua
    1 oz. rum

ALEXANDER
    1 oz. crème de cacao
    1 oz. brandy

ANGEL WINGS
    1 oz. crème de menthe
    1 oz. brandy

AMORE
    1 oz. amaretto
    1 oz. brandy

ROYALE
    1 oz. cognac
    1 oz. Grand Marnier

MEXICAN
    1 oz. Kahlua
    1 oz. tequila

IRISH EYES
    1 oz. Irish whiskey
    1 oz. Bailey's Irish Cream

IRISH NUT
    1 oz. Bailey's Irish Cream
    1 oz. Frangelico
    1 oz. Irish whiskey

HOMEMADE COFFEE LIQUEUR

Makes 1 quart

Store this easy-to-make liqueur in a dark place to age for two weeks before serving.

2 cups sugar
2 cups water
2 oz. instant coffee granules

$1\frac{1}{2}$ cups brandy or vodka
1 vanilla bean, cut in half lengthwise

Bring sugar and water to a boil, stirring to dissolve sugar. Add coffee and simmer for 3 minutes. Cool. Add brandy and vanilla bean. Pour into a bottle, seal and store at room temperature for two weeks. Strain out vanilla bean before serving.

IRISH CREAM LIQUOR

3 cups

Try this wonderful mixture in your next cup of after-dinner coffee.

1 cup Irish whiskey
4 eggs
1 tsp. vanilla extract

1 tbs. chocolate syrup
1 can (14 oz.) sweetened condensed milk
$\frac{1}{4}$ tsp. coconut extract

Combine ingredients in a food processor or blender. Store in the refrigerator.

THAI ICED COFFEE

My husband was with the U.S. Air Force in Thailand during the Vietnam war. For many years after he told me about the wonderful iced coffee. Finally Thai food became very popular in Seattle, and we were able to get authentic Thai coffee and produce the genuine article at home. Imagine our surprise when we read the ingredient label and found coffee, corn and sesame among the ingredients. We are positively addicted to this wonderful drink and enjoy it with everything from Equal and skim milk to cream and sugar!

4 oz. ground Thai coffee
cream
sugar
sweetened condensed milk

Use a drip coffee maker and grind coffee mixture to medium texture. In a 10-cup capacity coffee maker, brew as usual. Serve coffee over ice in a tall glass. Add cream and sugar to taste, or sweetened condensed milk. Store any remaining coffee in the refrigerator.

Thai coffee is available from Asian markets or online from **http://importfood.com/.**

MOOSE MILK

This recipe comes from the wilds of Canada: hence the name.

1½ qt. milk
1 qt. half-and-half
1 cup crème de cacao
1 cup Kahlua
1 fifth dark rum
½ gallon ice cream
nutmeg for garnish

In a large bowl, break ice cream into chunks. Pour other ingredients over the top and stir. Ladle into cups and dust with nutmeg.

APPETIZERS AND MAIN DISHES

COFFEE AND HAZELNUT CHICKEN

Serves 8–10

To prepare hazelnuts, toast in a 350° oven for 10 minutes, or until light golden brown. Place in a clean dish towel and rub to remove brown papery skins.

¼ cup oil
1 tsp. seasoning salt
½ tsp. ground black pepper
ten 5 oz. boneless, skinless chicken breasts

2 cups fine, dry breadcrumbs
¼ cup chopped toasted hazelnuts
¼ cup ground coffee

Mix oil, seasoning salt and pepper. Place chicken breasts in a shallow dish and pour oil mixture over. Turn to coat. In a shallow dish, combine breadcrumbs, nuts and coffee.

Dip each chicken breast into breadcrumb mixture. Place on a cookie sheet sprayed with nonstick cooking spray. Heat oven to 350°. Bake chicken breasts for 20 to 25 minutes, or until juices run clear when pierced with a fork. Prepare *Mushroom Cream Sauce,* page 29.

MUSHROOM CREAM SAUCE

$1/4$ cup butter
$1/4$ cup flour
3 cups heavy cream
3 tbs. butter

2 cups thinly sliced fresh mushrooms
1 tsp. salt
$1/2$ tsp. white pepper

Melt butter in a heavy-bottomed sauce pan over medium-high heat. When melted, whisk in flour and stir constantly for 1 minute. Gradually whisk in cream. Cook until mixture is thickened and smooth. Remove from heat and set aside. Melt butter in a large skillet and cook mushrooms until softened. Sprinkle with salt and pepper and stir into cream sauce. Pour over cooked chicken breasts.

COFFEE STEAK

This recipe is truly Seattle! It's a fun recipe to try for summer barbecues.

$^1/_2$ cup olive oil
$^1/_2$ cup Worcestershire sauce
3 cloves garlic, minced
16 oz. favorite steak, such as sirloin, rib eye or tenderloin

RUB
$^1/_3$ cup coarsely ground dark roast coffee
$^1/_2$ cup ground pepper
1 tbs. seasoning salt

Combine oil, Worcestershire and garlic. Coat steaks with sauce mixture and rub with coffee/pepper/salt mixture. Let sit for 30 minutes or cover and refrigerate from 2 hours to overnight. Heat grill and sear steaks. Cook to desired doneness.

COFFEE GLAZED HAM

This glaze also works well on turkey.

³/₄ cup strong brewed coffee
1 cup molasses
1 jar (12 oz.) apricot jam
2 tbs. cider vinegar
1 tbs. Dijon mustard
1 tsp. vanilla extract
one 8–9 lb. bone in, fully cooked ham

Combine coffee, molasses, jam, vinegar, mustard and vanilla until blended. Place ham in a lightly greased baking dish. Trim ham and score fat in a diamond pattern. Pour glaze over ham. Bake at 350° for 2 hours, basting ham every 20 minutes. If ham becomes too dark, cover loosely with foil.

COWBOY BEANS

Coffee adds a depth of flavor to these popular beans. These are delicious served with burgers or flour tortillas for a vegetarian entrée. Add a green salad and dinner is set.

2 tbs. olive oil
1 onion, chopped
1 green pepper, chopped
1 tbs. chopped garlic
2 bay leaves
2 tbs. chili powder
2 tsp. dried oregano

1 tsp. ground cumin
1½ cups water
1 can (8 oz.) tomato sauce
1 tbs. brown sugar
1 tbs. instant espresso powder
3 cans (15 to 16 oz each) pinto beans or
    chili beans, rinsed and drained

Heat oil in a large skillet. Cook onion, green pepper and garlic until softened. Add remaining ingredients and simmer over low heat for 45 minutes.

PORK SATAY

Thai in origin, this makes a fun appetizer for a summer evening. Satay are also good with chicken or beef.

2 lb. pork tenderloin
2 garlic cloves, minced
1 tbs. salad oil
2 tsp. chili powder
2 tsp. coriander

1 tsp. ginger
3 tbs. brown sugar
1 tbs. lemon juice
$1/4$ cup coffee

Slice pork $1/4$ inch thick and 1 inch wide. Combine all ingredients in a glass dish and marinate pork for several hours or overnight.

To prepare, remove pork from marinade and blot dry with paper towels. Thread on bamboo skewers. Broil or grill over hot coals until pork is cooked through, about 4 minutes on each side. Serve with *Peanut Sauce,* page 34, or plum sauce.

PEANUT SAUCE

This sauce is very complex in flavors and you can adjust the "heat" to suit your taste. It freezes well and is always a hit.

1 tbs. oil
1 onion, chopped
2 garlic cloves, minced
1 cup chunky peanut butter
1 cup coconut milk
½ cup milk
2 tbs. fish sauce or soy sauce
3 tbs. brown sugar

1 tbs. lemon juice
1 tbs. lime juice
3 bay leaves
¼ tsp. cinnamon
1 tsp. curry powder
½–1 tsp. chili paste or cayenne pepper, to
    taste

Heat oil in a large saucepan and sauté onion and garlic until soft. Add remaining ingredients and stir with a whisk until blended. Simmer for 5 minutes. Taste and adjust seasonings to your personal preference. Cool and remove bay leaves. Store in the refrigerator or freeze. This sauce goes well with chicken or beef satay.

PICADILLO

This makes a delicious appetizer served with tortilla chips. Or serve it over rice as a main course; pass sour cream, salsa, guacamole, shredded cheddar and sliced green onions to go on top.

1 cup raisins
1 cup hot coffee
2 lb. lean ground beef
2 onions, finely chopped
2 garlic cloves, minced
1 tbs. olive oil
2 tart apples, peeled, cored and coarsely
  chopped

1 cup chopped pimiento-stuffed green
  olives
1 can (14 oz.) stewed tomatoes
1 can (4 oz.) diced green chiles
salt and pepper to taste
1/2 tsp. cinnamon
1/2 tsp. cloves
1 cup slivered almonds, lightly toasted

Pour hot coffee over raisins and set aside to plump. In a large skillet, heat olive oil and sauté meat, onions and garlic until cooked. Drain off any excess liquid. Drain coffee from raisins; add raisins to meat mixture along with remaining ingredients, except almonds. Cook over medium heat for 10 minutes, stirring occasionally. Taste and correct seasoning. Stir in almonds and serve.

BEV'S BEST POT ROAST

Servings: 6–8

This unusual recipe for pot roast is similar to a variation of German sauerbraten. The vinegar tenderizes the meat overnight and adds flavor, while the coffee makes a rich base for gravy.

one 4 to 5 lb. chuck roast
4 garlic cloves
1 onion, sliced
1 cup raspberry vinegar

2 tbs. salad oil
2 cups brewed coffee
3 cups water

The day before serving, cut slits into meat and insert cloves of garlic into cuts. Place roast in a shallow bowl and top with onion slices. Pour vinegar over meat, cover and refrigerate overnight; turn occasionally.

The next day, remove meat from marinade and pat dry. Discard vinegar-onion mixture. Heat oil in a large roaster. Brown beef on both sides over medium high heat. Add coffee. Bake at 325° for 2 to 4 hours, or until meat is fork-tender.

If desired, add potatoes, carrots and onions around roast the last 45 minutes of cooking.

LAMB IN PITA

A nice casual supper. You can prepare the meat mixture and sauce the night before.

2 lb. lamb, cubed
1 tbs. oil
2 onions, chopped
2 carrots, chopped
1 garlic clove, minced
1 can (16 oz.) tomatoes, well drained
½ cup dark raisins
1 tbs. chili powder

1 tsp. curry powder
1 tsp. salt
1 tsp. sugar
½ tsp. cloves
½ tsp. cinnamon
½ cup coffee
salt and pepper to taste

In a large skillet, brown lamb in oil until brown. Add onion, carrots and garlic and cook until soft. Add remaining ingredients and cover. Simmer until tender, about 1 to 1½ hours. Split pita bread and fill with meat mixture. Serve with yogurt sauce.

YOGURT SAUCE

8 oz. unflavored yogurt
½ cucumber, seeded and diced

½ onion, chopped
2 tsp. dill

Combine ingredients and chill.

GUT-BUSTER CHILI

Servings: 8–10

The flavor of this zesty chili is even better if it is made the day before serving. Serve with shredded cheddar cheese, diced onion, cilantro and sour cream for topping.

4 lb. coarsely ground beef for chili
2 yellow onions, chopped
2 garlic cloves, minced
2 green peppers, cored, seeded and
   chopped
1 can (14 oz.) diced canned tomatoes
1 can (8 oz.) tomato paste
1 can (8 oz.) diced green chilies
2 cups brewed coffee

1/4 cup chili powder
3 tbs. cocoa powder
1 1/2 tbs. cumin
1/2 tsp. crushed red pepper
2 tsp. salt, or to taste
2 bay leaves
finely grated zest of one orange

In a large soup kettle, sauté beef, onion and garlic. Drain off excess liquid. Add remaining ingredients and simmer for 1 hour, until flavors are developed and mellowed.

HOLIDAY CHICKEN

Servings: 8

This recipe is also good with Cornish game hens.

4 whole chicken breasts, with bones and skin
¾ cup strong coffee
½ cup brandy
¼ cup salad oil
¼ cup honey

juice and zest of 1 lemon
¾ cup prepared mincemeat
1 tbs. cornstarch
2 tbs. water
parsley and orange slices for garnish

The day before you plan to serve this dish, divide chicken breasts in half and place in a shallow ovenproof casserole. Combine coffee, brandy, oil, honey, lemon juice and zest. Pour over chicken, cover and refrigerate overnight.

Heat oven to 375°. Pour off ¾ cup of the marinade. Bake chicken, uncovered, skin-side down, for 20 minutes. Turn skin side up and continue cooking for 10 to 20 minutes longer, until chicken is done. Test by making a small cut with a knife in the thickest part of one piece.

Place ¾ cup of the marinade in a small saucepan. Combine cornstarch and water; add to marinade. Bring to a boil over medium heat and stir in mincemeat. Whisk until heated through. Remove chicken to a large platter, pour sauce over and garnish.

BARBECUED BEEF

Servings: 8–12

Serve this spicy beef on toasted sourdough rolls. A big green salad makes a great accompaniment.

one 3–4 lb. eye-of-the-round roast

MARINADE

2 tbs. instant coffee
1/2 cup water
1/3 cup cider vinegar
1/4 cup salad oil
1 cup catsup
1 tsp. salt

1/2 tsp. pepper
1 tsp. chili powder
1 tsp. celery seed
2 garlic cloves, minced
4 drops Tabasco Sauce, or to taste

Combine marinade ingredients. Place trimmed beef in a large plastic bag and pour marinade over. Refrigerate overnight, turning occasionally. Remove beef from marinade and grill over medium coals for 45 to 60 minutes, or until meat tests rare with a meat thermometer, 140° when measured in the thickest part. To serve, thinly slice beef and serve on toasted rolls. May be served hot or cold. Spicy mustard and thinly sliced onions and dill pickles are good with this.

CHICKEN PAPRIKA

The coffee adds depth and richness to this recipe.

4 whole chicken breasts, halved
1 tsp. salt
1 tbs. paprika
½ cup butter
1 large onion, chopped
2 tbs. flour

1 tbs. paprika
1 cup coffee
3 tbs. tomato paste
¼ cup sherry
1 cup sour cream

In a plastic bag, combine salt and paprika. Add chicken to bag. Shake chicken until evenly coated. In a large skillet, brown chicken in melted butter. Remove chicken and place in an ovenproof casserole. In the drippings, sauté onion until soft. Blend in flour and paprika to form a paste. Add coffee and tomato paste and stir until blended. Add sherry and sour cream. Pour sauce over chicken. Cover tightly and bake at 350° for 1 hour. Serve with noodles.

MAHOGANY RIBS

Parboiling the ribs in water, garlic and a dash of cider vinegar tenderizes them and adds flavor while decreasing the cooking time.

4 lb. country-style spareribs
1 cup coffee
½ cup molasses
2 cloves garlic, minced
¼ cup Dijon mustard
3 tsp. Worcestershire sauce
½ cup cider vinegar
1 tsp. chili powder

Place ribs in a large pot and cover with cold water. Add ¼ cup cider vinegar and 1 tsp. garlic salt or powder. Bring to a boil, turn heat to low and simmer for 15 minutes. Drain well.

In a small saucepan, combine coffee with remaining ingredients. Simmer over low heat until blended. Place ribs in a shallow ovenproof casserole. Pour sauce over. Cover and bake at 325° for 1¼ hours or until tender.

COUNTRY HAM WITH RED EYE GRAVY

Servings: 4

In the true Southern tradition, this country ham is served with grits. The grits recipe is from Tom's mother and we all love it. If you're not fond of spicy food, use plain cheese instead of the jalapeno.

four ¼-inch slices country ham
1 cup water

2 tbs. black coffee

Cook ham slices in a heavy skillet over low heat until lightly browned, about 15 minutes. Remove and keep warm. Stir water and coffee into skillet. Bring to a boil and scrape up any brown bits from skillet. Serve gravy over ham and grits.

MARY'S GREAT GRITS

4 cups water
1 dash salt
1 cup grits
½ cup butter

2 eggs, beaten
1 tube Kraft Jalapeño Cheese Spread, or
about 1 cup of shredded cheddar
1 tsp. seasoning salt

Bring water to a boil in a saucepan. Add grits and stir to combine. Cook for 5 minutes over medium low heat. Add remaining ingredients and pour into a buttered casserole dish. Bake at 350° for 30 to 40 minutes.

GUSSIED UP BAKED BEANS

These go great with a family barbecue of burgers and hot dogs.

1/2 lb. bacon, diced
1 large yellow onion, chopped
2 cans (16 oz. each) baked beans
1/2 cup molasses
1/2 cup brewed coffee
1/2 cup brown sugar
1/4 cup catsup
1 tbs. mustard

Sauté bacon and onion until bacon is beginning to crisp and onion is limp. Drain off any excess fat. Combine with remaining ingredients in a large ovenproof casserole. Bake at 350° for 30 minutes, or until bubbly.

CITRUS-GRILLED RIBS

Servings: 6

Prepare sauce in advance to allow flavors to mellow. Try the sauce on any grilled meats.

6 lb. country-style pork ribs
3 tbs. oil
1/3 cup hoisin sauce
1/3 cup soy sauce
1 tbs. grated fresh ginger

3/4 cup whiskey
1/4 cup orange juice
1/4 cup grapefruit juice
1/4 cup brown sugar
2 tsp. fresh garlic, minced

Parboil ribs in water with a dash of cider vinegar and garlic salt. Simmer for 20 minutes and drain. Combine remaining ingredients and marinate ribs for 1 to 2 days in the refrigerator, turning occasionally. Drain ribs. Discard marinade. Barbecue and baste with *Coffee Barbecue Sauce.*

COFFEE BARBECUE SAUCE

Makes 3 cups

1 cup very strong coffee
1 1/2 cups catsup
1/2 cup Worcestershire sauce
1/2 cup dark brown sugar

1/3 cup cider vinegar
1 tsp. crushed garlic
1 tsp. chili powder

Combine all ingredients in a large saucepan. Simmer for 5 minutes. Cool and refrigerate.

CAKES, TORTES, CHEESECAKES, PIES AND CREPES

MOCHA CRÈME ROLL-UPS

This dessert is like eating a cloud!

5 eggs, separated
1 cup sugar
6 oz. German sweet chocolate
3 tbs. water

1 cup heavy cream
1 tbs. instant coffee
1/4 cup powdered sugar
1 tbs. powdered cocoa

Beat egg yolks with 3/4 cup of the sugar until thick and lemon colored. Melt chocolate with water. Cool. Stir chocolate into yolks. In a separate bowl, beat egg whites with an electric mixer, gradually adding remaining 1/4 cup sugar. Fold whites gently into egg and chocolate mixture. Heat oven to 300°. Butter an 11 x 15-inch jelly roll pan and line with parchment. Butter parchment. Spread batter evenly in pan. Bake at 300° for 15 minutes, turn oven to 350° and bake for 10 minutes.

Remove from oven and cover with a damp dish towel. Chill thoroughly. Remove towel and sprinkle heavily with cocoa. Turn over onto another sheet of parchment. Remove top piece of parchment. Whip cream with instant coffee and powdered sugar. Spread on top of cake. Roll up like a jelly roll, using the bottom paper as a guide. Chill. Cut into slices to serve.

JAMAICAN RUM CAKE

Servings: 12–18

Extremely rich, this wonderful dessert is only for the most dedicated dessert lovers! Rich rum cake is topped with coffee butter cream, spread with Chocolate Satin, page 70, and sprinkled with toasted almonds. The combination of flavors and textures is truly outstanding. This cake can be frozen.

RUM CAKE

½ cup butter
1 cup sugar
2 eggs
½ cup buttermilk
1 tsp. vanilla extract

1½ cups flour
1 tsp. baking powder
½ tsp. baking soda
½ tsp. salt

Heat oven to 350°. With an electric mixer, cream butter and sugar until light. Add eggs, buttermilk and vanilla. Sift together flour, baking powder, soda and salt. Add to egg mixture and combine. Pour batter into a greased and floured 9 x 13-inch baking pan. Bake for 35 to 40 minutes, or until cake tests done. While hot, poke holes in top of cake with a fork and pour *Rum Glaze* over the top while hot. Let cake cool completely and spread with *Coffee Buttercream*. Refrigerate.

Spread top of cake with *Chocolate Satin,* page 70. Use as much or as little of the topping as you desire and freeze the remainder to frost brownies or other desserts. Sprinkle top of cake with 1 cup toasted slivered almonds, if desired. Store cake in the refrigerator. Let warm slightly before serving. Cut into small squares.

RUM GLAZE

1 cup sugar
1/4 cup water
1/2 cup butter

3 tbs. dark rum—Meyers or Bacardi are
  good
1 tbs. vanilla extract

Combine sugar and water in a saucepan. Heat and bring to a boil. Add butter and stir until melted. Add rum and vanilla.

COFFEE BUTTERCREAM

1/2 cup butter
4 oz. white chocolate, melted
1/4 cup powdered sugar

1 tbs. instant coffee
1 tsp. hot water
2 eggs

Using the steel knife of a food processor or an electric mixer, combine butter, melted white chocolate and powdered sugar until smooth. Dissolve coffee in hot water. Add to butter mixture along with eggs. Process until smooth.

SPICE CAKE

Moist and flavorful, this cake keeps well.

1 pkg. yellow cake mix
1 pkg. (3¾ oz.) instant butterscotch pudding
4 eggs
½ cup vegetable oil
1 cup brewed coffee

1 tsp. cinnamon
1 tsp. nutmeg
½ tsp. allspice
1 cup raisins
1 cup chopped pecans

Heat oven to 350°. Combine all ingredients except raisins and nuts and beat with an electric mixer for 5 minutes. Add nuts and raisins. Pour into a greased and floured bundt pan. Bake for 45 to 50 minutes or until cake tests done. Cool for 15 minutes; turn out onto a wire rack and cool completely.

CREAM CHEESE ICING

1 pkg. (8 oz.) cream cheese
2 cups powdered sugar
¼ cup butter

1 tsp. vanilla extract
brewed coffee to thin

Using the steel blade of a food processor, combine cream cheese, butter, powdered sugar and vanilla. Add coffee to thin to spreading consistency. Frost cake.

JAVA POUND CAKE

This delicious coffee-flavored cake freezes well.

1 cup butter
1¼ cups sugar
4 eggs
½ cup brewed coffee
2¼ cups flour
1 tsp. baking powder
½ tsp. salt
2 tsp. vanilla extract
½ tsp. mace

Heat oven to 325°. Using an electric mixer, cream butter and sugar until light and fluffy. Add eggs, beating well after each addition. Add coffee and vanilla. Sift dry ingredients together and add to creamed mixture. Pour into a well greased 9 x 5-inch bread pan lined with parchment paper on the bottom. Bake for 1 hour and 25 minutes, or until cake tests done. Cool in pan for 15 minutes and then turn out onto a rack to cool completely.

COFFEE PECAN CHEESECAKE

Servings: 8–12

You'll love the combination of flavors in this rich, light-textured cheesecake.

CRUST

1 cup finely ground pecans   2 tbs. butter
1/4 cup sugar

Combine ingredients and press into the bottom of a 9-inch springform pan. Bake at 350° for 10 minutes. Cool.

FILLING

1 pkg. unflavored gelatin   2 tsp. vanilla extract
3 tbs. Meyer's dark rum   1 tbs. instant coffee
11 oz. cream cheese, softened   3 tbs. hot water
1 cup powdered sugar   1 cup whipping cream

In a small saucepan, soften gelatin in rum. Place over low heat and dissolve. Cool slightly. Using the steel blade of a food processor, mix cream cheese with powdered sugar and vanilla. Dissolve coffee in hot water and add to cream cheese mixture. Add softened gelatin and blend. In a separate bowl, whip cream until soft peaks form. Combine cream cheese mixture with whipped cream. Pour into prepared crust. Chill. Garnish.

MOCHA CHOCOLATE CHIP CHEESECAKE

For best results, always refrigerate a cheesecake overnight before serving.

CRUST

6 tbs. butter, melted   2 tbs. sugar
1½ cups chocolate wafer crumbs

Combine ingredients. Press onto bottom and partially up sides of a buttered 10-inch spring-form pan. Bake at 350° for 10 minutes. Cool while making filling. Turn oven temperature to 200°.

FILLING

1½ lb. cream cheese, room temperature   1 tsp. vanilla extract
1 cup sugar   ⅓ cup heavy cream
4 eggs, room temperature   6 oz. mini semisweet chocolate chips
1 tbs. instant coffee powder

Using the steel knife of a food processor, combine cream cheese and sugar until light. Add eggs and process until smooth. Scrape down sides of bowl. Add instant coffee and vanilla and combine. Pour half of the filling into prepared crust. Stir chocolate chips into remaining filling and carefully pour over filling in pan. Bake for 2 hours, until set. Cool at room temperature. Cover with plastic wrap and refrigerate overnight.

CAPPUCCINO CHEESECAKE

Servings: 8–12

My sister-in-law, Joanna, and I have been cooking together for years, both professionally and personally. She is a firm believer in the mixer, while I prefer the Cuisinart. In a side-by-side test making cheesecakes one day, we made one in the mixer and the other in the food processor. The texture and creaminess of the food processor cheesecake won hands down.

CHOCOLATE CRUMB CRUST

1 tbs. butter
1 pkg. (9 oz.) dark chocolate wafer
   cookies, finely ground
1 pinch cinnamon
1/3 cup melted butter

Coat bottom and sides of a 9-inch spring-form pan with 1 tbs. butter. In a food processor, using the steel blade, combine cookie crumbs, cinnamon and melted butter. Press crumb mixture evenly on sides and bottom of prepared pan. Bake at 325° for 5 minutes. Cool.

FILLING

1¼ lb. cream cheese, cut into 1-inch cubes
1¼ cups sugar
4 eggs, beaten
¾ cup whipping cream
¾ cup sour cream
1 oz. finely chopped semisweet chocolate
¼ cup espresso coffee
3 tbs. Kahlua
1 tsp. vanilla extract

Using the steel blade of a food processor, combine cream cheese, sugar and eggs until smooth. Scrape sides down and add whipping cream and sour cream. Process to combine. Melt chocolate with espresso in the microwave and cool. Add chocolate mixture and liqueur to cream cheese mixture. Pour into prepared crust.

Bake at 325° for 75 minutes, or until sides of cake are set 2 inches in from edges and center of cake is still pudding-like. Remove cake from oven and let cool on a wire rack to room temperature. Refrigerate cake overnight.

PEANUT BUTTER TORTE

Servings: 8–12

This is fantastic with coffee. The addition of molasses gives the peanut butter more depth.

CRUST

1 cup graham cracker crumbs
1 cup chocolate wafer crumbs
1/4 cup sugar

1/4 cup melted butter
1/4 cup peanut butter

Mix ingredients together and press into the bottom of a springform pan.

FILLING

8 oz. cream cheese
1 cup sugar
1 cup creamy peanut butter

1 tbs. molasses
1 tbs. vanilla extract
1 cup heavy cream, whipped

Beat cream cheese with sugar until light and fluffy. Add peanut butter, molasses and vanilla. Fold in whipped cream. Pour into prepared crust and smooth top. Cover and chill.

TOPPING

4 oz. semisweet chocolate, melted

2 tbs. butter

2 tbs. oil

½ cup chopped salted peanuts

Melt chocolate with butter and oil, stirring to combine. Cool slightly and spread on top of chilled torte. Sprinkle with chopped peanuts and refrigerate. To serve, cut into wedges with a hot knife.

TOFFEE ICE CREAM TORTE

Servings: 8–12

This is quick, easy to make and delicious. Be sure to pass extra sauce at the table.

1 cup almond macaroon crumbs
2 tbs. melted butter
1 qt. chocolate ice cream, slightly softened
1 cup fudge sauce
1 qt. coffee ice cream, slightly softened
4 Heath toffee bars, coarsely chopped

Combine crumbs and butter and press into bottom of a 9-inch springform pan. Bake at 350° for 8 to 10 minutes, or until golden. Cool. Spread chocolate ice cream evenly on crust, drizzle with chocolate sauce and freeze until firm. Spread with coffee ice cream and sprinkle with chopped toffee. Drizzle with remaining fudge sauce. Cover and freeze until firm.

To serve, remove from freezer several minutes before slicing. Cut into wedges with a hot, wet knife.

ICE CREAM MERINGUE TORTE

Servings: 8

Often walnuts that are sold in packages at the grocery store have rubbed together and much of their skins have come off. When using walnuts in baking, you will get a much nicer result if you take the time to place walnuts in a strainer and rinse them thoroughly with warm water. Shake to remove excess water and toast them briefly at 300° for 5 minutes; then proceed with your recipe.

3 egg whites, room temperature
1 cup sugar
22 Ritz crackers, crushed
1/2 tsp. baking powder

3/4 cup chopped walnuts
1 tsp. vanilla extract
coffee ice cream
chocolate sauce for topping

Using an electric mixer, beat egg whites until foamy. Add sugar gradually, beating until stiff. Fold in crackers, baking powder, nuts and vanilla. Butter a 9-inch pie pan.

Heat oven to 325°. Pour mixture into prepared pan and bake for 30 minutes. Cool. To serve, cut into wedges and place a scoop of ice cream in the center. Top with chocolate sauce.

CASSATA

This rich Sicilian dessert uses purchased pound cake to speed preparation.

1 purchased pound cake
1 lb. ricotta cheese
2 tbs. whipping cream
1/4 cup sugar
2 tbs. Grand Marnier liqueur

1/2 cup chopped candied fruit, such as
    cherries and orange peel
2 tbs. finely chopped toasted almonds,
    hazelnuts or pistachio nuts
2 oz. chopped semisweet chocolate

Trim ends off cake and slice it horizontally into fourths. In a food processor workbowl or blender container, combine ricotta, cream, sugar, liqueur, fruit, nuts and chocolate. Place bottom layer of cake on a serving platter and spread with 1/3 of the cheese mixture. Repeat layers of cake and cheese, ending with cake. Refrigerate until firm, about 2 hours. Frost tops and sides. Decorate with remaining frosting. Cover and refrigerate for 24 hours before serving, for flavors to mellow. Slice to serve.

FROSTING

12 oz. semisweet chocolate
1/2 cup strong brewed coffee

1 cup butter

Melt chocolate with coffee. Beat with an electric mixer, adding butter a piece at a time. Chill to spreading consistency.

KAUAI PIE

Hawaii's version of the mainland's Mud Pie.

COCONUT CRUST

1½ cups butter cookie crumbs
½ cup flaked coconut

¼ cup melted butter
1 tsp. vanilla extract

Mix crust ingredients together and press into a 9-inch pie pan. Bake at 375° for 10 minutes and cool.

FILLING

½ gallon coffee ice cream
1 cup fudge sauce

2 cups macadamia nuts
½ cup flaked coconut

Soften ice cream slightly. Rinse macadamias if you wish to rid them of excess salt. Toast briefly at 375° for 5 minutes. Chop coarsely. Spread half of the ice cream in bottom of prepared crust. Drizzle with half of the fudge sauce, half of the nuts and coconut. Repeat. Wrap and freeze until serving. To serve, thaw at room temperature for 10 to 15 minutes and cut into wedges.

KONA BANANA CREAM PIE

Servings: 8

Whenever you make a graham cracker pie crust, add a teaspoon of vanilla—it improves the flavor immensely!

MACADAMIA NUT CRUST

1/4 cup macadamia nuts
1 cup graham cracker crumbs
1/4 cup sugar

1/4 cup butter, melted
1 tsp. vanilla extract

Using the steel knife of a food processor, combine crust ingredients. Press into a 9-inch pie plate. Bake at 375° for 10 minutes. Cool.

FILLING

3/4 cup sugar
5 tbs. flour
1/4 tsp. salt
1 cup coffee

1 cup evaporated milk
1 egg beaten with 1 tsp. milk
1 tsp. vanilla extract
3 bananas

In a heavy-bottomed saucepan, stir together sugar, flour and salt. Add coffee and evaporated milk. Bring to a gentle boil, whisking frequently, until mixture begins to thicken. In a small bowl, beat egg, milk and vanilla. Add ¼ cup of the hot mixture to bowl, stirring constantly. Add egg mixture to the pan and stir constantly until mixture thickens. Remove from heat and cool.

Slice 1 banana into bottom of prepared crust. Pour half of cooled pudding mixture into crust, and top with another sliced banana and remaining pudding. Slice the last banana on top and spread with *Whipped Cream Topping.* Chill.

WHIPPED CREAM TOPPING
1 cup heavy cream
½ cup powdered sugar
1 tsp. instant coffee
¼ cup chopped macadamia nuts

In a small bowl, whip cream. Add sugar and coffee. Spread on pie and sprinkle with nuts.

TOFFEE PIE

This pie recipe has been popular for years. For a decorative touch, garnish with chocolate-covered coffee beans.

PIE SHELL

1 cup flour
$1/2$ tsp. salt
$1/2$ cup shortening
$1/3$ cup brown sugar
$3/4$ cup finely chopped pecans
1 oz. grated unsweetened chocolate
1 tbs. ice water

Combine flour and salt. Cut in shortening until mixture resembles coarse crumbs. Add brown sugar, nuts and chocolate. Sprinkle with ice water and mix well. Pat into a 9-inch pie pan. Bake at 375° for 15 minutes. Cool.

FILLING

¾ cup butter, room temperature	2 tsp. instant coffee powder
1 cup plus 2 tbs. sugar	3 eggs
1½ oz. unsweetened chocolate, melted and cooled	

Beat butter with an electric mixer until creamy. Gradually add sugar, beating until light. Blend in chocolate and coffee. Add eggs, one at a time, beating for 3 minutes after each addition. Pour into cooled pie shell. Refrigerate for several hours or overnight.

TOPPING

1 cup heavy cream
1 tsp. instant coffee powder
¼ cup powdered sugar
1 oz. unsweetened chocolate, grated

Combine cream, coffee and confectioners' sugar in a bowl. Refrigerate for several hours. Beat together until stiff and spread on top of pie. Grate chocolate over top.

CREPES BRÛLOT

Cafe Brûlot is a spiced hot coffee drink with strips of lemon and orange peel, which is often flamed tableside. It's a specialty of New Orleans. This dessert is a spin-off of that popular drink.

COFFEE CREPE BATTER   Makes 16 crepes

1 cup flour   1 tbs. sugar
1½ cups milk   2 tsp. instant coffee
3 eggs

Blend all ingredients together and strain through a wire mesh sieve. Heat a 6-inch crepe pan or skillet and brush with oil. On medium high heat, pour about 2 tbs. of the batter into the pan. Lift and twirl skillet to spread. Brown on one side and turn to lightly cook other side. Repeat procedure using remaining batter. Stack crepes using waxed paper to separate.

FILLING

8 oz. cream cheese

1/4 cup powdered sugar

1 tbs. milk

1 tbs. Grand Marnier or brandy

1 tbs. grated orange zest

1 tsp. grated lemon zest

Combine ingredients until light and fluffy. Spread on prepared crepes and roll up cigar fashion. Place in a shallow ovenproof casserole. Refrigerate for several hours or overnight.

SAUCE

1/2 cup sugar

2 tbs. cornstarch

2 cups strong brewed coffee

1 tsp. cinnamon

1/4 tsp. cloves

1 tsp. orange zest

1 tsp. lemon zest

1/3 cup brandy

whipped cream for garnish, optional

ice cream for garnish, optional

In a saucepan, mix together sugar and cornstarch. Stir in coffee and cook over medium heat, stirring occasionally, until thickened. Add spices and zest. Pour sauce over crepes and bake at 325° until heated through, about 10 to 15 minutes. In a small pan, heat brandy, ignite and pour over crepes. Place crepes on dessert plates, allowing 2 crepes per person. Garnish with whipped cream or ice cream if desired.

SCRUMPTIOUS STUFF CHOCOLATE CREPES WITH KAHLUA MOUSSE

Servings: 12

My friend Sandy is the creator of this elegant recipe that not only tastes delicious but can be made ahead and frozen. She used to have her own catering company called Scrumptious Stuff—and it was.

CHOCOLATE CREPES
Makes 24 crepes

4 eggs
1½ cups milk
1 cup flour
¼ cup unsweetened cocoa

¼ cup sugar
2 tsp. vanilla extract
¼ cup melted butter

Combine ingredients in a blender or using the steel blade in a food processor. Pour batter through a sieve into a pitcher. Heat a crepe pan or skillet over medium high heat and brush lightly with oil. Pour a small amount of the batter into pan. Lift and twirl skillet to spread. Cook on one side and turn to cook lightly on other side. Repeat procedure using remaining batter. Stack crepes using waxed paper to separate.

KAHLUA MOUSSE

6 egg yolks
1/2 cup sugar
1 tbs. Kahlua

2 tsp. instant coffee
3 cups semisweet chocolate chips, melted
1 1/2 cups heavy cream, whipped

Using an electric mixer, beat egg yolks, sugar, Kahlua and coffee until light. Fold in melted chocolate and whipped cream.

TO ASSEMBLE

Spread several spoonfuls of mousse onto one edge of each crepe and roll up cigar-fashion. Place in a shallow container and separate layers with waxed paper. May be refrigerated or frozen at this point. If frozen, thaw in the refrigerator before serving. To serve, place two crepes on a pretty dessert plate and garnish with a flower or serve with whipped cream or a sauce. Sauces which go well include hot fudge, raspberry, *Crème Anglaise*, page 116, or *White Chocolate Sauce*, page 116.

CHOCOLATE SATIN

This recipe is very versatile in that it can be baked and served as a very rich torte, or be used unbaked as a filling or frosting. Don't attempt to make it without a food processor.

8 oz. unsweetened chocolate
4 oz. semisweet chocolate
½ cup water

1⅓ cups sugar
1 cup butter, cubed
5 large eggs, room temperature

Heat oven to 350° and butter a 9-inch cake pan. Line with baking parchment and butter paper. Place sugar and water in a small saucepan and bring to a boil. Stir until sugar dissolves. In a food processor, using the steel blade, combine chocolates and chop finely. With the machine running, add boiling sugar syrup, scraping sides of work bowl. With the machine running, add eggs and butter, processing until mixture is smooth and satiny.Pour batter into prepared pan and bake for 25 minutes. Cool. Serve cut in wedges with whipped cream, raspberry sauce or *Crème Anglaise,* page 116. Can also be used as a filling or frosting. Refrigerate or freeze any leftover.

BREADS, MUFFINS AND COFFEE CAKES

BEST EVER CINNAMON ROLLS

Makes 12 rolls

We love the hint of orange in these delightful rolls, just the thing to start your morning right with your favorite cup of coffee.

DOUGH

2 pkg. active dry yeast
1/4 cup warm water
3 tbs. sugar
1 1/2 cups buttermilk

4 1/2 cups flour, divided
1 tsp. salt
1/2 tsp. soda
1/2 cup oil

Using the steel blade of a food processor, combine yeast, water and sugar. Process briefly and let stand 5 minutes. Heat buttermilk to lukewarm. Add to work bowl along with half of the flour. Process to combine, letting the machine run for 1 minute. Add salt, soda, oil and remaining flour to the work bowl. Process to make smooth dough. Place dough in an oiled bowl and cover. Let rise 15 minutes.

FILLING

³/₄ cup butter, melted

2 cups brown sugar

2 tsp. cinnamon

zest of 2 oranges

Combine filling ingredients. Roll dough out on a lightly floured surface into a rectangle approximately 10 x 18 inches. Spread filling on dough. Roll up lengthwise and cut into twelve 1½-inch pieces. Place cut side up in a buttered 9 x 13-inch pan. Let rise for 30 minutes.

Heat oven to 400°. Bake rolls for 10 to 15 minutes, until lightly browned. Turn upside down onto a serving platter. Glaze if desired. Serve warm.

GLAZE

4 oz. butter

3 oz. cream cheese

2 cups powdered sugar

juice of 2 oranges

Combine butter, cream cheese and powdered sugar adding orange juice until mixture is of spreading consistency. Drizzle onto warm rolls.

FOOD PROCESSOR BLACK BREAD

This hearty bread goes wonderfully with soups. I've been making bread in my food processor for years and have always been pleased with the results. If your machine seems unable to handle the dough, just finish it by hand and increase kneading time. This recipe can be doubled.

1 cup warm water (115°)
1 pkg. active dry yeast
1 tsp. sugar
1½ cups flour
1 tsp. salt
1 cup whole bran cereal
½ cup strong coffee
2 tbs. distilled vinegar
2 tbs. molasses
1 oz. unsweetened chocolate, melted
2 tbs. butter
2–2½ cups rye flour, divided
1–2 tbs. caraway seeds

Using the steel blade of the food processor, combine water, yeast and sugar. Process a few seconds and let yeast proof for 5 minutes. Add 1½ cups flour and let the machine run for several minutes to activate gluten in flour.

Add salt, bran, coffee, vinegar, molasses, chocolate, butter and half of the rye flour. Let machine run until a stiff dough forms. Add caraway seeds and remaining flour until dough forms a ball. Remove dough from workbowl and knead on a floured board until dough is smooth and elastic. Put dough into an oiled bowl and turn to coat. Cover with a damp towel and let rise in a warm place until doubled.

Punch down dough and shape into a ball. Place in a greased 8-inch round cake pan and let rise in a warm place until doubled, about 1 hour. Heat oven to 350°. Bake loaf for 45 minutes or until it sounds hollow when tapped on the bottom.

Prepare glaze: Mix 1 tsp. cornstarch with ⅓ cup water and brush on top of loaf. Return to oven for 3 minutes longer. Remove from pan and cool on a wire rack.

BANANA BREAD

This recipe is unusual in that it uses olive oil: it makes an exceptionally moist banana bread. To make sour milk, pour 3 tbs. regular milk in a glass measuring cup, add 1 tsp. lemon juice or white vinegar and let stand for 5 minutes. I usually use walnuts for the nuts here.

3 large, overripe bananas, mashed
2 eggs, beaten
1/3 cup extra light olive oil
3 tbs. sour milk
1 cup sugar

2 cups flour
1 tsp. baking soda
1/2 tsp. salt
1 cup chopped nuts, optional

Heat oven to 325°. Grease two 3 x 7-inch bread pans. Using an electric mixer or food processor, combine wet ingredients. Using a wire mesh strainer, sift dry ingredients into mixture and combine. Add nuts, if desired. Divide evenly into prepared pans and bake for 45 minutes to 1 hour, until banana bread tests done with a wooden pick. Cool on a wire rack. Wrap in foil and refrigerate overnight before serving.

BUTTER PECAN MUFFINS

This recipe is different as the batter is prepared the night before and refrigerated overnight, which makes these ideal for weekend brunches.

½ cup butter
1 cup brown sugar, firmly packed
1 egg
1 cup milk
½ tsp. soda
1 tsp. vanilla extract
2 cups flour
½ cup chopped pecans

Generously grease a 12-cup muffin tin. Mix ingredients together using an electric mixer. Pour into prepared tin. Cover with plastic wrap and refrigerate overnight.

Heat oven to 400°. Bake muffins for 30 minutes or until done.

MOCHA CHIP MUFFINS

These are just the thing for a Sunday morning treat.

$\frac{1}{2}$ cup butter
$\frac{1}{2}$ cup brown sugar
$\frac{1}{2}$ cup granulated sugar
2 tbs. instant coffee
2 tsp. vanilla extract
2 eggs

1 cup milk
1$\frac{3}{4}$ cup flour
$\frac{1}{2}$ tsp. salt
1 tbs. baking powder
1 cup semisweet chocolate chips
1 cup chopped walnuts

Heat oven to 350°. Cream butter, sugars, coffee and vanilla until light and fluffy. Beat together eggs and milk. Sift together flour, salt and baking powder. Add wet ingredients and dry ingredients to butter mixture, stirring just to combine. Add chips and nuts. Line twelve 3-inch muffin cups with paper liners or grease and flour well. Divide batter evenly into muffin tins. Bake for 20 to 25 minutes.

Servings: 8–12

...able in 6 oz. bags in the baking section. Or if you ...th or Skor candy bars.

1 cup pecans, chopped
1 tsp. baking soda
1 cup buttermilk
1 egg, beaten
1 tsp. vanilla extract

...x 2-inch baking dish. Using an electric mixer, com-...ixture resembles coarse meal. Remove 1/2 cup of the ...e with toffee and pecans for topping. Add soda to ...nbine. Stir in buttermilk, egg and vanilla. Pour into ...ut mixture. Bake for 35 minutes or until a toothpick ...Cool. Cut into squares to serve.

COCONUT SOUR CREAM COFFEE CAKE

Servings: 12

Sour cream makes this cake rich and tender.

1 cup butter
2 cups sugar
3 eggs
1 cup sour cream
1 tsp. vanilla extract
2 cups flour
1 tsp. baking powder

½ tsp. salt
1½ cups coconut

FILLING
1 cup chopped pecans
4 tsp. cinnamon
⅓ cup brown sugar
¾ cup coconut

Heat oven to 325°. Grease and flour a bundt pan. Using an electric mixer, combine butter, sugar and eggs until light. Add sour cream and vanilla. Sift flour, baking soda and salt. Add to creamed mixture. Stir in coconut.

To make filling, combine pecans, cinnamon, brown sugar and coconut in a small bowl.

Spoon ⅓ of cake batter into prepared pan. Sprinkle with ½ of the filling. Repeat, ending with cake batter. Bake for 1¼ to 1½ hours, or until cake tests done.

UP ALL NIGHT COFFEE CAKE

Fortunately it's the cake that stays up all night—not you. This is so convenient to make the night before a special weekend breakfast. Either instant or regular pudding mix works well.

3/4 cup chopped pecans
1 pkg.(3 3/4 oz.) butterscotch pudding mix, dry
1/2 cup brown sugar
1/2 cup butter, melted
2 tsp. cinnamon
1 pkg. (3 lb.) frozen bread dough rolls

Butter a 10-inch tube pan or bundt pan well. Sprinkle with chopped nuts. Combine dry pudding mix, sugar, butter and cinnamon. Arrange rolls in the pan. Sprinkle with pudding mixture, distributing it evenly. Cover top of pan with plastic wrap and place in a cold oven overnight. In the morning, remove rolls from the oven and heat oven to 350°. Return rolls to the oven and bake for 25 minutes.

MOCHA COFFEE CAKE WITH COFFEE GLAZE

Servings: 12–16

This has just the right touch for a special brunch on Sunday morning. Be sure to feature plenty of freshly brewed coffee to go with—we particularly like Sulawesi Indonesian blend.

BATTER

3/4 cup butter
1 1/2 cups sugar
2 tsp. vanilla extract
3 eggs
3 cups flour

1 1/2 tsp. baking powder
1 1/2 tsp. baking soda
1/2 tsp. salt
2 cups plain yogurt

Heat oven to 350°. Prepare *Filling* and set aside.

Grease and flour a 10-inch tube pan or bundt pan and set aside.

With an electric mixer, cream butter and sugar until light and fluffy. Stir in vanilla. Add eggs one at a time, beating well after each addition. Sift together dry ingredients and add 1/3 at a time, alternating with yogurt. Batter will be very thick.

Pour 1/4 of the batter into prepared pan and sprinkle with 1/3 of the filling. Repeat twice, ending with batter. Bake for 1 hour or until toothpick inserted in the center comes out clean. Cool on a wire rack. Frost with *Coffee Glaze* and sprinkle with chopped walnuts, if desired.

FILLING

¾ cup brown sugar

¾ cup raisins

¾ cup chopped walnuts

2 tbs. cocoa

1 tbs. cinnamon

2 tsp. instant coffee powder

Combine filling ingredients in a small bowl.

COFFEE GLAZE

1 tsp. instant coffee

1 tbs. hot water

6 tbs. butter

4 oz. cream cheese

¾ cup powdered sugar

1 tsp. vanilla extract

1 tsp. orange juice

pinch of salt

To make glaze, combine coffee powder in hot water. Beat butter and cream cheese until light. Add cooled coffee mixture and cream cheese, beating until light and fluffy. Add vanilla, orange juice and salt. Beat until very light. Spread decoratively on top and sides of cake. Sprinkle with nuts if desired.

DESERTS

85 Mocha Pecan Pie
86 Chocolate Patê
87 Boule de Neige
88 Triple Chocolate Bavarian
90 Kahlua Flan
91 Chocolate Bliss
92 Frozen Espresso Mousse
93 Coffee Pots de Crème
94 Brandied Coffee Velvet
95 Amaretto and Kahlua Semifreddo
96 Coffee Almond Tortoni
97 Espresso Tiramisu
98 Cricket's Authentic Tiramisu
100 Coffee Coeur la Crème
101 Coffee Fromage
102 Poached Pears With Mocha Sabayon

MOCHA PECAN PIE

This pecan pie has a richness and depth that make it particularly delicious. The mini chocolate bits are a nice surprise. Serve it with whipped cream flavored with Kahlua and a teaspoon of instant espresso powder.

one 9-inch refrigerated pie crust
3 tbs. butter, melted
2 tbs. cocoa powder
1/4 cup heavy cream
1 tbs. instant espresso powder
1 cup light corn syrup

1 cup sugar
3 eggs, beaten
2 tsp. vanilla extract
1/4 tsp. salt
1 1/2 cups pecans
1 cup mini semisweet chocolate chips

Heat oven to 350°. Place crust in pie pan. In a medium bowl, combine butter, cocoa powder, cream and espresso. Stir in corn syrup, sugar, eggs, vanilla and salt. Add pecans and chocolate chips. Bake for 1 hour, or until center is set. Cool. Serve with Kahlua-flavored whipped cream.

CHOCOLATE PATÊ

This dessert is ideal for large parties as it can be made weeks in advance and frozen. We enjoy it with a raspberry sauce, Crème Anglaise, *page 116,* White Chocolate Sauce, *page 116, or a bit of whipped cream.*

1 pint heavy cream
3 egg yolks
½ cup light corn syrup
16 oz. semisweet chocolate, chopped

½ cup butter
⅓ cup powdered sugar
1 tsp. vanilla extract

Line a loaf pan with plastic wrap. Combine ½ cup of the cream with egg yolks in a heavy 3-quart saucepan. Stir in corn syrup, chocolate and butter. Cook over medium heat, stirring until chocolate is melted. Continue to cook for an additional 3 minutes, stirring constantly.

Remove from heat and cool to room temperature. Whip remaining cream with powdered sugar and vanilla. Fold evenly into chocolate mixture. Pour into prepared pan. Wrap well and freeze. To serve, slice across loaf and serve with sauce of your choice.

BOULE DE NEIGE

Boule de Neige means snowball in French. To garnish, pipe rosettes of whipped cream over the entire surface, or simply swirl whipped cream in a decorative fashion.

12 oz. semisweet chocolate, chopped
3/4 cup freshly brewed strong coffee
1 cup sugar
1 1/2 cups butter

6 eggs, beaten
1 pint heavy cream for garnish, whipped
  and sweetened to taste

Heat oven to 300°. Line a 2-quart stainless steel mixing bowl with a single piece of heavy duty foil. Spray with non-stick cooking spray. Make sure there are no tears in the foil.

Melt chocolate with coffee and sugar in a heavy saucepan over medium heat. Stir until sugar is dissolved. Add butter in pieces, whisking to combine. Remove from heat and quickly stir in beaten eggs. Immediately strain mixture into prepared bowl. Place in lower third of oven and bake for 60 to 65 minutes. It will rise, crack and become crusty and dry around edges. Let cool at room temperature; then refrigerate overnight. Dessert will firm as it cools.

To serve, turn upside down onto a plate. Peel off foil and trim edges to make a nice shape. Frost with whipped cream. Chill until serving. To serve, cut into wedges with a hot knife, wiping the blade between slices.

TRIPLE CHOCOLATE BAVARIAN

Servings: 8

Admittedly this recipe takes a bit of skill, but the results are worth it. Read the directions thoroughly and make it the day before your dinner party when you have a bit of extra time.

1 tbs. unflavored gelatin
¼ cup cold water
5 egg yolks
½ cup sugar
1 cup half-and-half, scalded
3 oz. white chocolate, grated
3 oz. milk chocolate, grated
3 oz. semisweet chocolate, grated
1 tsp. instant coffee powder
1½ cups heavy cream, whipped

Brush the inside of a 6-cup soufflé dish with vegetable oil. Soften gelatin in cold water and set aside. Beat egg yolks in sugar with a mixer until pale yellow and mixture forms a ribbon when the beaters are lifted. Gradually whisk half-and-half into yolk mixture.

Transfer yolk mixture to a saucepan and cook, stirring constantly, until mixture thickens and coats a spoon, about 10 to 12 minutes. Remove from heat and whisk in softened gelatin, stirring thoroughly until gelatin completely dissolves.

Place each of the grated chocolates into its own separate bowl. Add 1/3 of the yolk mixture to each bowl and whisk until chocolate melts. Add coffee powder to the semisweet chocolate mixture. Refrigerate each mixture.

Whip cream until stiff. Fold 1/3 of the whipped cream into each of the chocolate mixtures. Pour white chocolate mixture into oiled dish. Tap to eliminate air bubbles. Cover and freeze for 10 minutes to set layer. Repeat steps with milk chocolate layer and then semisweet chocolate. Cover and refrigerate for 4 hours or overnight.

To serve: Rub bottom and sides of soufflé dish with a hot damp towel and invert onto a lightly oiled plate. Cut into wedges. Serve with a raspberry or mocha fudge sauce. Serve immediately.

KAHLUA FLAN

This makes a delightful dessert for a Mexican meal—or any meal.

2 cups sugar
1/4 cup water
8 eggs

1/2 cup sugar
3 1/2 cups whole milk
1 cup Kahlua liqueur

Heat 2 cups of sugar and water in a small saucepan over medium high heat for 25 minutes or until sugar is golden brown. Pour caramelized sugar into a shallow glass baking dish, such as a pie plate or ceramic quiche dish.

Beat together eggs, sugar, milk and Kahlua until well blended. Pour into prepared pan.

Heat oven to 250°. Place flan in a larger baking pan and fill half way up the sides with boiling water. This is called a *bain marie* or water bath. Bake flan for 45 to 60 minutes, or until custard is set.

Chill completely. To serve, spoon custard into individual bowls and drizzle with caramel. Garnish with fresh berries and a sprig of mint if desired.

CHOCOLATE BLISS

The combination of chocolate, cream cheese and almond is really bliss!

1 cup sugar
1/2 cup butter
4 eggs
1 1/2 tbs. sour cream

1 1/2 tbs. vanilla extract
1/2 tsp. salt
1 cup flour
16 oz. semisweet chocolate, melted

Heat oven to 350°. Using an electric mixer, combine sugar, butter, eggs, sour cream and vanilla until smooth. Add salt and flour. Melt chocolate and add to mixture. Pour into a 9- or 10-inch springform pan lined with parchment paper.

TOPPING

16 oz. cream cheese
1/2 cup butter
2 eggs

1 cup sugar
2 tbs. almond extract

Combine ingredients using the steel blade of a food processor or an electric mixer. Pour cream cheese mixture on top of chocolate mixture and run a knife through both batters, creating large swirls and giving a marbled effect.

Bake for 20 to 30 minutes or until set. Cool completely and store in the refrigerator.

FROZEN ESPRESSO MOUSSE

Try using different liqueurs, such as amaretto, Frangelico or crème de cacao to change the flavor of this smooth dessert. Rum or brandy are very good too. This is a nice dessert for a dinner party as it must be made ahead.

1 tbs. instant coffee
1 tbs. hot water
4 eggs, separated

$\frac{1}{2}$ cup sugar
1 cup whipping cream
3 tbs. Kahlua

Dissolve coffee in hot water and set aside. Beat egg yolks until thick and lemon colored. In a separate bowl, beat egg whites until stiff, adding sugar gradually until glossy. In another bowl, beat cream until stiff. Blend in coffee mixture and liqueur. Fold all three mixtures together gently to combine. Pour into an attractive freezer-proof mold. Cover and freeze. To serve, scoop into small bowls.

VARIATIONS

- Garnish with a rosette of whipped cream and a chocolate-covered coffee bean.
- Serve with hot fudge sauce or chocolate sauce.
- Place individual servings in pretty coffee mugs or demitasse cups before freezing.

COFFEE POTS DE CRÈME

You can make superfine sugar at home by processing regular granulated sugar in the food processor with the steel blade.

2½ cups heavy cream, divided
3 tbs. instant coffee
2 tsp. vanilla extract
6 egg yolks

½ cup superfine sugar
2 tbs. powdered sugar
cinnamon

Scald 2 cups of the cream in a heavy saucepan. Stir in coffee and vanilla. In a separate bowl beat egg yolks and superfine sugar until thick and lemon colored. Gradually pour cream into egg mixture, beating constantly.

Heat oven to 325°. Bring a pan of water to a boil. Place 6 individual *pots de crème* cups in a shallow pan. Divide cream mixture evenly into them. Pour boiling water half way up the sides to form a *bain marie* or water bath. Carefully place in oven and bake for 35 minutes. Cool and refrigerate for 3 hours before serving.

Just before serving, whip remaining ½ cup cream with powdered sugar. Use to garnish tops of *pots de crème* and dust each with cinnamon.

BRANDIED COFFEE VELVET

This is wonderful for after dinner.

2 tbs. instant coffee
¼ cup hot water
¼ cup chocolate syrup
½ cup brandy
1 qt. rich vanilla ice cream
whipped cream for garnish

Dissolve coffee in hot water. Add remaining ingredients and combine until smooth. Chill. Pour into frosted glasses to serve and garnish with whipped cream.

AMARETTO AND KAHLUA SEMIFREDDO

This wonderful dessert must be made ahead. Semifreddo never freezes completely solid and the contrast in temperatures between cold dessert and hot fudge sauce is fantastic.

2 cups heavy cream
1 cup powdered sugar
4 egg whites

¼ cup amaretto liqueur
¼ cup Kahlua liqueur
2 tbs. instant coffee

Prepare a long narrow freezer-proof container, such as a bread pan, by lining with plastic wrap. In a bowl, whip cream until beginning to thicken, slowly adding powdered sugar. In a separate bowl, whip egg whites until soft peaks form. Fold the two mixtures together. Divide mixture into 2 bowls. Add amaretto to first bowl. Pour into prepared pan and smooth into an even layer. Place in freezer until beginning to set. Dissolve coffee in 1 tsp. hot water. Add coffee and Kahlua to second bowl. Carefully spread on top of amaretto layer. Cover with plastic and freeze for several hours or overnight. To serve, cut into slices and serve drizzled with warm fudge sauce.

VARIATION

Stir crushed amaretti cookie crumbs into the amaretto layer and grated semisweet chocolate into the Kahlua layer.

COFFEE ALMOND TORTONI

This is a nice dessert for an Italian meal.

1 cup heavy cream
½ cup sugar, divided
1 tsp. vanilla extract
½ tsp. almond extract

2 egg whites, room temperature
½ cup finely chopped toasted almonds
½ cup flaked toasted coconut
1 tsp. instant coffee powder

Line 8 muffin cups with paper liners. Combine cream with ¼ cup of the sugar, vanilla and almond extract and beat until soft peaks form.

In a separate bowl, beat egg whites, gradually adding remaining sugar, until stiff. Fold in whipped cream and ½ of the nuts and coconut. Spoon half of the mixture evenly into muffin tins, smoothing top with the back of a spoon. Add coffee powder to remaining whipped cream mixture and spoon an even layer over top of tortoni. Sprinkle tops with remaining almonds and coconuts. Cover and freeze until serving.

ESPRESSO TIRAMISU

Tiramisu means "pick-me-up" in Italian. Mascarpone is a sweet Italian cream cheese. This is a shortened version of this popular dessert.

3/4 cup Kahlua
2 cups espresso
50 lady fingers
3 3/4 cups mascarpone cheese

2 1/2 cups heavy cream
1 cup sugar
1/2 cup cocoa powder

Combine Kahlua and espresso in a large bowl. Dip lady fingers in mixture and use them to line bottom and sides of a 10-inch springform pan, arranging them in an attractive design. You will use about 1/3 of the lady fingers.

Using the steel blade of a food processor, combine mascarpone, cream and sugar until it begins to thicken.

Spread 1/3 of the cheese mixture over the bottom of the pan. Layer again with liqueur-soaked lady fingers. Repeat layers twice, ending with cheese mixture. Dust top with cocoa powder. Cover and chill for at least 3 hours or overnight. Remove sides from pan. Cut into wedges to serve.

CRICKET'S AUTHENTIC TIRAMISU

Servings: 12

My friend Cricket, who studied cooking in Italy, presents her version of this wonderful dessert. A challenging recipe, but worth the effort and calories involved.

PAN DI SPAGNA (SPONGE CAKE)

4 large eggs, separated
1 tsp. vanilla extract
3/4 cup sugar

1/2 cup flour
1/2 cup cornstarch
pinch of salt

Heat oven to 350°. Butter a 9- or 10-inch cake pan that is 2 inches deep, and line with parchment. Using a mixer, beat egg yolks with vanilla for 5 minutes. Sift flour and cornstarch together. In a separate bowl, using an electric mixer, beat egg whites and salt until they hold a firm peak. Fold yolks into whites. Sift flour and cornstarch into egg mixture in 3 additions. Do not overmix. Pour batter into prepared pan, smoothing top. Bake for 30 to 40 minutes, or until cake tests done. Gently invert onto a wire rack and cool.

ESPRESSO SYRUP

1/3 cup sugar
1/4 cup water

1/2 cup very strong brewed espresso
1/4 cup brandy

Combine sugar and water in a saucepan and bring to a boil. Cool. Add espresso and brandy. Set aside.

ZABAGLIONE FILLING

3 large egg yolks
1/3 cup sugar
1/3 cup sweet Marsala wine

1/2 pound mascarpone cheese, room
    temperature
2/3 cup heavy cream, whipped

Using an electric mixer, beat egg yolks, sugar and marsala until light. Set bowl over a pan of simmering water and continue beating until thickened, about 10 minutes. Whip mascarpone until smooth. Fold together egg mixture, Mascarpone and whipped cream.

To assemble: Cut sponge cake into 1/4-inch vertical slices. Place a layer of slices (about 1/3 of the cake) in a shallow 2-quart dish. Soak with 1/3 of the espresso syrup. Spread with 1/2 of the filling. Repeat layers of cake, syrup, filling, cake and syrup. Spread with topping.

TOPPING

1 cup heavy cream, whipped
2 tbs. sugar
ground cinnamon

ground coffee
unsweetened cocoa powder

Whip cream and sweeten with sugar. Decorate top of tiramisu and dust with cinnamon, coffee and cocoa. Refrigerate for several hours before serving.

COFFEE COEUR LA CRÈME

An unusual twist on the traditional Coeur la Crème. Serve this rich cheese spread with English biscuits, plain cookies or fresh fruit.

16 oz. cream cheese, softened
1 cup heavy cream; whipped
½ cup sour cream
2 tbs. instant coffee
1 tbs. boiling water
3 tbs. powdered sugar

Blend softened cream cheese with whipped cream. Stir in sour cream. Dissolve coffee in water and add to mixture along with powdered sugar. Line a pretty mold with damp cheese cloth and fill with cheese mixture. Chill for several hours or overnight. Unmold onto a dessert plate and garnish with fresh flowers.

COFFEE FROMAGE

This is a rich, whipped molded dessert from Norway, very much like a Bavarian cream. Garnish with whipped cream and fresh fruit such as oranges, bananas, strawberries, raspberries or peaches.

1 envelope unflavored gelatin
3 tbs. water
3 eggs
¾ cup sugar

2 tbs. instant coffee powder
1 cup heavy cream
fresh fruit for garnish
sweetened whipped cream, for garnish

Soften gelatin in water. Stir over hot water or microwave until dissolved. In the large bowl of an electric mixer, beat eggs until light. Add sugar and instant coffee. Beat at high speed for 5 minutes or until very thick.

Whip cream until stiff. Add dissolved gelatin. Fold mixture into beaten eggs and beat at lowest speed of mixer until well combined. Pour into a 5-cup dessert mold and chill until set, about 4 hours or overnight.

To serve, dip mold into warm water and loosen edges with a knife. Unmold onto a pretty dessert plate and garnish with fresh fruit and whipped cream.

POACHED PEARS WITH MOCHA SABAYON

Servings: 6

The combination of chilled fresh pears and rich warm sauce is wonderful!

6 ripe Bartlett pears, with stems
3 cups water
1 cup sugar

1 piece lemon rind
1 stick cinnamon

Peel pears, leaving stems on. In a large saucepan, combine water, sugar, lemon and cinnamon. Bring to a boil and add pears. Cover and gently poach until just tender. Test in fattest part of pear, using the tip of a small knife. Let pears cool in syrup. Refrigerate until chilled.

SABAYON SAUCE

4 oz. semisweet chocolate
3/4 cup strong coffee
9 egg yolks

5 tbs. sugar
1 1/4 cup brandy

Melt chocolate with 1/4 cup of the coffee; set aside. In the top of a double boiler, mix egg yolks with sugar. Beat with an electric mixer until pale yellow. Do not underbeat! Gradually add chocolate and remaining coffee to egg mixture, stirring over simmering water until creamy and thickened. Add brandy. Place pears in individual dishes and spoon sauce over.

COOKIES, CONFECTIONS AND SAUCES

MOCHA MELTAWAYS

Similar to Naniamo Bars, these rich bars literally melt in your mouth.

CRUST

1½ cups graham cracker crumbs
1½ cups chocolate wafer crumbs
1 cup chopped walnuts

½ cup melted butter
¼ cup sugar
1 tbs. vanilla extract

Combine ingredients and press into the bottom of a 9 x 13-inch pan. Chill.

MOCHA BUTTERCREAM

½ cup butter
1 cup powdered sugar
2 eggs

4 oz. white chocolate, melted
1 tbs. instant coffee
1 tsp. hot water

Using the steel blade of a food processor, or an electric mixer, combine butter and powdered sugar until smooth. Add eggs and melted white chocolate. Dissolve coffee in hot water and add to mixture. Spread on prepared crust.

Top with a layer of *Chocolate Satin,* page 70. Freeze any extra topping for another recipe. Store in refrigerator or freeze. Cut into bars to serve.

FUDGE FROGGIES

These delectable bars are a cross between fudge and a brownie. They are our all-time favorite brownie.

1 lb. semisweet chocolate chips
1 cup butter, cut in pieces
1/3 cup strong brewed coffee
4 large eggs, room temperature
1 1/2 cups sugar
1/2 cup flour
2 cups coarsely chopped walnuts

Melt together chocolate, butter and coffee. In an electric mixer, beat eggs and sugar until light. Slowly add chocolate mixture. With a spoon, stir in flour and walnuts.

Heat oven to 375°. Line a 9 x 13-inch baking pan with foil. Generously butter foil. Pour batter into prepared pan. Bake for 30 minutes or until just set around edges. Cool on a wire rack for 30 minutes. Cover pan with foil and refrigerate for several hours or overnight.

Cut into bars to serve. These bars are best stored in the refrigerator.

MOCHA ALMOND FLORENTINES

Servings: 30

Using disposable aluminum cake or tartlet pans makes clean up easy. The technique is a bit time-consuming but the results are worth it.

1 cup butter
1 cup sugar
6 tbs. honey
6 tbs. heavy cream

1 lb. slivered blanched almonds
3 tsp. instant coffee
1 tsp. hot water
12 oz. semisweet chocolate

Heat oven to 375°. Spray six 8-inch round foil cake pans or thirty 3-inch tartlet pans with non-stick cooking spray. In a heavy saucepan, combine butter, sugar, honey and cream. Bring to a boil over medium heat, stirring frequently. Cook at a boil for 1½ minutes, stirring constantly. Remove from heat and add almonds. Divide mixture evenly into prepared pans, using your fingers dipped in cold water to flatten. If using individual tartlet pans, place them on cookie sheets. Bake for 10 to 12 minutes, or until golden around the edges. Let cookies cool in the pans; they will harden as they cool. Place pans in the freezer for 10 minutes. Remove cookies by tapping and gently pressing on backs of pans.

Combine instant coffee and hot water. Melt chocolate and stir in coffee mixture. With a spoon, spread chocolate on the back of each cookie. Place upside down on wire racks to harden. Store in refrigerator or freezer.

ESPRESSO SHORTBREAD

If you wish, melt semisweet chocolate and dip each cookie one third of the way up in the melted chocolate. Press a blanched almond or pecan half in the center of each.

1 cup butter
1/2 cup brown sugar, firmly packed
1 tsp. vanilla extract
3/4 tsp. instant coffee
2 1/4 cups flour
1/4 tsp. salt

Cream butter and sugar until fluffy. Add vanilla and coffee. Combine flour and salt and add to mixture. Chill dough.

Heat oven to 325°. Roll dough to 1/4-inch thickness. Cut into bars 1 inch wide and 3 inches long. Prick with a fork. Place on greased cookie sheets and bake for 20 to 25 minutes, or until golden.

OLD-FASHIONED MOLASSES SPICE COOKIES

Makes 1 dozen

This treasured family recipe has been handed down through the generations by Helen Louise Thwing. She was nice enough to share it with us. Try it in your lunch box—it makes a big batch.

1 cup butter
1 cup brown sugar
1 cup molasses
2 eggs
1 cup strong coffee
1 lb. dark raisins
4 cups flour

1 tbs. each cinnamon, ground cloves, ginger
1 tsp. nutmeg
$\frac{1}{4}$ tsp. allspice
$1\frac{1}{2}$ tsp. baking soda
1 tsp. salt

In a large mixing bowl, cream butter, brown sugar, molasses and eggs until fluffy. Pour hot coffee over raisins and let plump. Stir together flour, spices, baking soda and salt. Add to creamed mixture. Combine with undrained raisins. Heat oven to 350°. Drop dough by rounded teaspoons onto greased baking sheets. Bake for 15 minutes. Cool on wire racks. If desired, frost with *Browned Butter Icing.*

BROWNED BUTTER ICING

½ cup butter
3 to 4 cups powdered sugar
1 tsp. vanilla extract

In a saucepan, heat butter until just beginning to brown. It should give off a very "nutty" aroma. Remove from heat and add powdered sugar until spreading consistency. Stir in vanilla. Spread on cooled cookies.

MOCHA MACADAMIA NUT COOKIES

Makes 1 dozen

These flavorful cookies are similar to chocolate chip cookies, with the addition of coffee, macadamia nuts and white chocolate chips. Be sure to chill the dough well and don't overbake.

1 cup butter
1¾ cups brown sugar
2 eggs
½ cup brewed strong coffee
3½ cups flour
1 tsp. baking soda

½ tsp. salt
1 tsp. nutmeg
½ tsp. cinnamon
1 cup semisweet chocolate chips
1 cup white chocolate chips
1 cup macadamia nuts

Cream butter, sugar, eggs and coffee until fluffy. Sift flour, soda, salt and spices and add to mixture. Stir in chips and nuts. Chill dough well for at least 1 hour.

To bake, heat oven to 400°. Drop dough by rounded spoonfuls onto greased baking sheets. Bake until edges are light brown, about 8 to 10 minutes. Remove to wire racks to cool. Store in a covered container.

MEXICAN MOCHA BALLS

These delightful little cookies are similar to the familiar Mexican tea cakes or wedding balls.

1 cup butter
½ cup sugar
1 tsp. vanilla extract
2 cups flour
1 tsp. instant coffee

½ tsp. salt
1 cup chopped walnuts
½ cup chopped maraschino cherries, well
   drained

Combine butter, sugar and vanilla. Add flour, coffee and salt. Stir in walnuts and cherries. Chill dough for 1 hour. Form chilled dough into 1-inch balls and place on an ungreased cookie sheet. Heat oven to 325°. Bake cookies for 20 minutes. Cool on a wire rack. Roll in powdered sugar and store in an airtight container.

MOCHA MADELEINES

These charming little cookies are perfect for an afternoon tea.

melted butter for molds
2 oz. semisweet chocolate
1/2 cup butter
2 eggs
1/4 cup sugar
1 tsp. vanilla extract
1 tsp. instant coffee

1 tsp. hot water
1/2 tsp. brandy
1/2 cup cake flour
2 tsp. cocoa
1/2 tsp. baking powder
powdered sugar

Heat oven to 325°. Brush madeleine molds with butter. Melt chocolate with 1/2 cup butter. Beat eggs with sugar until thick. Add melted chocolate mixture, vanilla, coffee, water and brandy. Stir in flour, cocoa and baking powder, mixing until flour just disappears. Spoon batter into prepared molds, filling 2/3 full. Bake for 10 to 12 minutes, or until a toothpick inserted in the center comes out clean. Loosen cookies and invert over a cake rack. Cool to room temperature. Dust with powdered sugar sprinkled through a sieve. Arrange the cookies on your prettiest plate and garnish with flowers.

ORANGE ALMOND BISCOTTI

Biscotti are baked twice. The key to success is not to bake them too long the first time, so they will slice nicely for the second baking. I can't imagine why people buy expensive biscotti when they are so easy and fun to do at home.

$\frac{1}{2}$ cup butter
1 cup sugar
2 eggs
1 tsp. orange zest
1 tsp. almond extract

$1\frac{3}{4}$ cups flour
$\frac{1}{2}$ tsp. salt
$1\frac{1}{2}$ cups ground almonds
1 cup whole almonds, blanched, toasted
  and coarsely chopped

Heat oven to 350°. Cream butter, sugar, eggs, orange zest and almond until light and fluffy. Stir in flour, salt and nuts. Dough will be soft. On a floured board with floured hands, shape dough into four 1-inch logs. Use additional flour as needed. Transfer logs to greased cookie sheets, leaving 3 inches of space between logs.

Bake logs for 10 to 12 minutes, until firm. Do not overbake. Remove sheets from oven. Turn oven to 275°. As soon as logs are cool enough to handle, cut on a 45° angle into $\frac{1}{2}$-inch slices using a bread knife. Return to baking sheet and bake for 10 minutes, or until biscotti are dry. Transfer to wire racks to cool.

FOOD PROCESSOR TRUFFLES

These make a nice gift from your kitchen at holiday time. A variety of liqueurs and coatings can be used. This recipe makes about 40 one-inch truffles. For the adventuresome, you can even try hand-dipping these in melted chocolate. Be sure to let the truffles sit at room temperature for 30 minutes before eating, so they will develop their full flavor and aroma.

½ pound semisweet chocolate chips
½ cup strong brewed coffee
1 tbs. butter
1 tbs. liqueur of choice (amaretto, Kahlua, Frangelico, kirsch, rum, brandy or other)
½ cup unsweetened cocoa, chocolate coffee beans, candied citrus, chopped nuts or other

Using the steel blade of a food processor, chop chocolate very fine. Heat coffee until just below boiling. With machine running, pour coffee down the feed tube. Add butter and liqueur and scrape sides of the work bowl. Continue processing until well combined and smooth. Place processor bowl in the refrigerator and chill until mixture is firm enough to be shaped.Form into small balls using a melon ball scoop, a teaspoon or your hands. Roll in cocoa. Store in a covered container, well sealed, in the refrigerator for up to 2 weeks. This may be frozen for up to 3 months.

COFFEE ICE CREAM BONBONS

These are something special to offer with after-dinner coffee. Experiment with using other liqueurs and flavors of ice cream.

1 tbs. unflavored gelatin
2 tbs. water
3 tbs. Kahlua or other liqueur
1 qt. coffee ice cream, softened
4 oz. semisweet chocolate chips
1 oz. vegetable shortening

In a small saucepan, soften gelatin in water and dissolve over low heat. Cool and add liqueur. Using an electric mixer, combine ice cream and gelatin mixture. Pour into a metal pan and freeze for several hours or overnight.

To form bonbons, chill a cookie sheet in the freezer. Using a melon baller, quickly form small ice cream balls. Place on chilled cookie sheet and insert a frilled toothpick into each. Return bonbons to freezer until firm.

Melt chocolate and shortening, stirring well. Pour into a coffee cup and cool slightly. Dip ice cream balls into chocolate, coating thoroughly. Return to freezer.

WHITE CHOCOLATE SAUCE

Makes 1½ cups

Perfect as a sauce for Chocolate Pâté, *page 86. For a change of pace use Grand Marnier or Frangelico instead of Kahlua. This sauce keeps well.*

1 cup heavy cream
9 oz. white chocolate, grated

½ cup Kahlua

Scald cream and remove from heat. Whisk in white chocolate. Pour into a food processor fitted with the steel blade and process until smooth. Add liqueur.

CRÈME ANGLAISE

2½ cups

This rich custard sauce may be flavored with your favorite liqueur or finely chopped toasted macadamia nuts or almonds.

2 cups heavy cream
6 egg yolks
½ cup sugar

1 pinch salt
2 tbs. liqueur of your choice, optional

Heat cream in a saucepan but do not boil. Whisk together egg yolks, sugar and salt until light yellow. Add cream and mix to blend. Pour mixture into a double boiler and cook until thickened. Add liqueur if desired.

MOCHA FUDGE SAUCE

Makes 1 cup

This sauce can easily be doubled. Store leftovers in a jar in the refrigerator. Try it over Amaretto and Kahlua Semifreddo, page 95. Today's food stylists often serve the dessert on top of the sauce or drizzle sauce over the top in a zig zag pattern.

3 tbs. butter
3 oz. unsweetened chocolate
1/2 cup strong coffee
1/4 cup light corn syrup
1 cup sugar
1 tsp. vanilla extract

In a saucepan, melt butter and chocolate. Stir in coffeee, corn syrup and sugar. Bring sauce to a boil and continue boiling gently, without stirring, until thick and smooth, about 10 minutes. Add vanilla. Serve sauce immediately or store in the refrigerator.

PART II – TEA

TEA HISTORY, PRODUCTION AND VARIETIES

For centuries, people all over the world have found comfort, communication and warmth in a simple cup of tea. The traditions, ceremonies and politics of tea have impacted civilization throughout history. In this section, you will find lots of information about tea, as well as recipes we find particularly good with tea. So whether you're enjoying a solitary cup or planning a festive party, you'll find something delicious to go with your next cup.

THE HISTORY OF TEA

Next to water, tea is the most popular drink in the world. Its history dates back almost 5,000 years. Although no one knows for certain how tea drinking began, legend has it that the Chinese Emperor, Shen Nung, was drinking hot water under a tree one day when a leaf from a nearby bush drifted into his cup. One sip and he was hooked! Supposedly this took place around 2737 B.C. At that time, tea leaves were dried, powdered and stirred into hot water. They were also made into cakes and added to boiled rice with spices and nuts. It wasn't until the Ming Dynasty, 1368 to 1644 A.D., that tea leaves were brewed as an infusion, as we know it today.

Tea was introduced to Japan by Buddhist priests in 593 A.D. It was the Dutch who brought green tea from Japan to Europe in the early 1600s. Initially it was sold for medicinal purposes and as an expensive drink, enjoyed only by the very wealthy. In the late 1700s the economy changed, reducing the price so that tea could be enjoyed by all.

In America, tea was the beverage of choice until the Revolution. When the British passed the Tea Act of 1773 the Colonists boycotted tea completely. A group of Colonists, dressed as Indians, threw tea from three ships into the harbor in what is known as the Boston Tea Party.

After the revolution tea became popular again, and the trade between China and America flourished. Great fortunes were made as ships from the Atlantic ports sailed around Cape Horn to the Pacific Northwest. There they loaded their ships with furs to trade in the Orient for tea, silk and spices.

Both iced tea and the tea bag are fairly recent American inventions. Iced tea was first served at the World's Fair in St. Louis in 1901. Temperatures were soaring, and when an enterprising tea salesman poured tea over ice, the crowds loved it. We've been drinking iced tea ever since, and today over 80 percent of the domestic tea market in the United States is served as iced tea.

In New York in 1908 another enterprising tea salesman began sending his samples to retailers in small silk bags. Assuming the tea was to be steeped in the bags, the retailers put them right into their pots. They loved the convenience of the premeasured, self-straining bags and ordered more!

Today, Americans use over 200 million pounds of tea per year. Most of it comes from China, India and Sri Lanka. The United Kingdom imports almost twice that amount.

HOW TEA IS GROWN

The tea plant is a member of the camellia family. It is an evergreen which grows in tropical and subtropical climates. Tea plants need rain in order to flourish. A climate with 50 inches of annual rainfall is ideal for growing tea. Much as the grapes used to make wine take on certain characteristics of the soil and climate, the tea plant also takes on a distinct flavor from the climate and soil in which it is grown. For example, a tea plant growing in India will taste completely different if transplanted to China.

If left unpruned, a tea plant will grow to a height of over 50 feet. Most plants are pruned, trained and clipped to a flat surface for ease in picking and are about four feet tall. Pruning also keeps the bush from going to seed and keeps it in a vegetative state where it produces new leaves year after year. A tea plant may remain productive for over a century!

Most tea plants are propagated by cuttings. Tea is a monoculture—that is, a crop grown in the same location year after year—so fertilizing is very important to maintain a healthy crop. On a typical tea estate there are usually 3000 to 5000 bushes per acre. Each acre yields 1000 to 2000 pounds of leaf per year.

The young leaf shoots and the unopened leaf buds of the tea plant are responsible for the smell and taste of the tea. There are two categories of picking: fine and coarse. These refer to the size of the shoot that is plucked. Two leaves and a bud are considered fine plucking and three or more is considered coarse. High quality teas are always harvested with fine plucking of the premium leaves. Tea is plucked or harvested at least three times a year, and in some climates it is a continual process. The frequency of picking depends on the number of new growths or flushes as they are called. There is a delicate balance between the frequency and the fineness of plucking, fertilizing and pruning in order to produce the maximum growth and quality.

Picking tea is almost always done by hand. A large tea estate will employ several hundred workers. It takes 2000 to 3000 shoots to produce one pound of tea. The average worker will pick about 800 pounds of tea per year.

TEA PROCESSING

All tea falls into one of three categories: green, black or oolong. These divisions are based solely on the methods of processing the tea leaf. Virtually all Japanese tea is green, almost all Indian tea is black, and China produces all three. Most Americans prefer black teas.

Green tea uses the simplest process. Shortly after the leaves are plucked, they are steamed or heated to stop the enzymatic action. The leaf is softened by the heat and then rolled various ways—balled, flat, curly, thin or twisted.

Drying reduces the moisture content of the leaf, preventing any further chemical changes.

When brewing, boiling water meets the tea and releases the natural fragrance and flavor that were stabilized during the steaming and drying process.

Black teas are dried out so that they lose about half of their moisture content. This process is called withering. The fresh green leaves are spread out on tiered racks of heavy cloth. Another method involves placing the leaves in a wire mesh trough. If the climate is not too wet or humid, the leaves dry naturally. Otherwise, huge fans are used. After the leaves are withered, they are taken to huge rolling machines. These machines twist and roll the leaves, breaking down their cellular structure and releasing the juices. The enzymatic action begins and the leaves darken. Then the leaves are broken up by coarse seives, or roll breakers. Next the leaves move to the fermenting rooms, where they are spread out to ferment and develop their full fragrance. This takes anywhere from twenty minutes to three hours. Briefly, this step occurs when the enzymes and oxygen combine to give the tea leaves their bright color. It also mellows the flavor of the juices, which prior to this point have been astringent and bitter. After the fermentation, the leaves are dried in huge chambers until they turn black and have a moisture content of about 5%.

Basically, this is the key distinction between green teas and black teas: green teas are called unfermented and black teas are called fermented.

Oolong teas are prepared much like black tea but are given only the briefest withering period and are only partially oxidized. Thus they share some of the same characteristics of both green and black teas.

THE SORTING AND GRADING OF TEA

Grading tea is a matter of size rather than quality of the leaves. After the black and oolong teas are dried, they are sorted into grades by machines. Different sizes are separated by vibrating wire mesh screens. It's important that the tea be consistent in size as smaller pieces brew more quickly than large ones. The two grades of tea are leaf grades and broken grades.

- Leaf grades include: souchong, pekoe and orange pekoe.
- Broken grades include: broken pekoe souchong, broken pekoe, broken orange pekoe, fannings and dust.

Green tea is graded according to the age of leaves and preparation. Some of the varieties include gunpowder, imperial and hyson.

VARIETIES OF TEA

Teas are often named for the area in which they are grown, such as Ceylon or Kenya. As many as 20 or 30 different teas will go into a blend. Here are some of the most common varieties:

- **Blended teas.** Various teas are combined to enhance a particular characteristic or flavor. Earl Grey, English Breakfast and China Caravan are familiar examples of blended tea.
- **Scented and flavored teas.** Teas which have been enhanced by flowers, natural oils or

fruits. Jasmine, Lychee, Lemon and Almond are popular varieties.

- **Chais and spiced teas.** Chai tea has recently become increasingly popular. Chai is usually made with black tea, cardamom, cinnamon or other spices, milk, and a sweetener. Other spiced teas are flavored with cinnamon or other combinations of spices.

- **Herbal teas.** Often these mixtures contain no tea at all, but are infusions or tisanes of various flowers, leaves, stems and herbs. Certain herbs are thought to have medicinal properties, such as chamomile for sleep or ginseng for potency.

- **Decaffeinated tea.** Water is the preferred method by which to decaffeinate tea. The chemicals used to decaffeinate coffee are restricted by law for use in decaffeinating tea. Sometimes ethyl acetate is used, but it adversely effects the tea.

THE PROPER POT, OR HOW TO BREW TEA

A perfect cup of tea begins with your favorite high quality tea. Use fresh cold tap water. Bring the kettle to a rolling boil. Heat your teapot by rinsing with very hot tap water. Purists bring the pot to the kettle, never the kettle to the pot. Pour the water directly onto the tea. Cover with the lid and let the tea steep for 3 to 5 minutes. Tea releases its color long before its flavor, so its color is no indication of the proper strength. If the resulting brew is too strong for your personal liking, use less tea or add more hot water.

Just before pouring, stir the tea to evenly distribute the flavor. Any tea left in the pot for longer than 10 minutes will develop an off flavor if the leaves are not removed. Either remove the leaves using a perforated spoon or strain into another warmed teapot.

To add milk to tea is a matter of continuing debate. In England it is common practice. Milk is only used with black tea, never green tea or oolong. The milk neutralizes the tannins in the tea and reduces the astringency. Cream should never be used in tea as the fat content changes the flavor. Some like a bit of lemon, sugar or honey in their tea, but it is mostly a matter of personal taste.

Be sure to keep your teapot clean, but avoid using a detergent that might leave a residue. The best way to clean a teapot is to fill it with hot water and a tablespoon of baking soda and let it stand for several hours.

TEA BEVERAGES

BASIC CHAI TEA

Makes 2 cups

Because chai tea is made with a lot of Oriental spices, it is easy to vary and fun to experiment with. Adjust the amounts of spice to your taste, or try adding mint, fennel, ginger, cloves or other spices as you wish.

1 1/2 cups water
1/2 cup milk (2% or greater fat content preferred)
2 tbs. sugar, or to taste
1/4 tsp. ground cardamom
1 small cinnamon stick
1/4-inch piece fresh ginger, chopped
1 1/2 tbs. black tea

Combine all ingredients except black tea in a small saucepan. Bring to a boil and remove from heat. Add tea and steep for 3 to 5 minutes. Strain and serve immediately.

QUICK CHAI TEA

Chai masala is available commercially at Indian stores and some specialty stores. It contains a ground combination of cardamom, cinnamon, black pepper and cloves. It is like the Indian spice blend garam masala, but without cumin added. Chai masala may also be sold as 'tea masala' or 'tea spice.' You can easily grind your own.

1 1/2 cups water
1/2 cup milk
2 tbs. sugar, or to taste
1/2 tsp. chai masala powder
1 1/2 tbs. black tea

Combine all ingredients except black tea and heat over the stove. Bring to a boil and remove from heat. Add tea and steep for 3 to 5 minutes. Serve immediately.

LIME TEA

This is a refreshing beverage to serve with a Mexican meal.

2 cups boiling water
2 tbs. loose black tea
1/2 cup sugar
2 1/2 cups ginger ale

2 1/2 cups lemon lime soda
peel from two limes
1/2 cup lime juice
1/2 cup corn syrup

Pour boiling water over tea and steep for 5 minutes. Strain. Add sugar and lime skins and let stand for 1 hour. Remove skins from tea and add remaining ingredients. Serve chilled over ice.

MAUI ICED TEA

On vacation in Hawaii, we picked up several new recipes which we wanted to share.

2 qt. brewed tea
1 cup orange juice
1 cup lime juice

1 cup pineapple juice
1/2 cup guava juice
sugar to taste, start with 1/3 cup

Combine all ingredients and serve over ice.

SPECIAL ICED TEA

This is a nice make-ahead drink to have on hand for those hot summer days.

2 cups water
2 cups sugar
1 qt. hot water
8 tea bags

2 qt. cold water
2 cups orange juice
3/4 cup lemon juice
orange slices and mint sprigs for garnish

Combine 2 cups water and sugar in a large saucepan and boil for 5 minutes. Remove from heat and add 1 quart hot water and tea bags. Steep tea bags for 3 to 5 minutes, according to taste. Add cold water, orange and lemon juice. Refrigerate or serve immediately over ice. Garnish each glass with a slice of orange and a sprig of fresh mint.

GINGER TEA

Try this for a change of pace.

4 slices ginger root, 1/4-inch thick
1/4 cup light brown sugar

6 cups boiling water

Bruise ginger slices with the flat side of a large knife blade. Place ginger in a teapot and add sugar and water. Steep 5 minutes.

PARTY PUNCH

This refreshing punch is perfect for a patio or backyard party.

4 cups strong brewed tea, such as Earl Grey
1 tsp. whole cloves
4 cups brewed mint tea
1 qt. pineapple juice
1 qt. orange juice
1 qt. apple juice
½ cup lemon juice
2 liters ginger ale
1 fifth light rum
fresh mint sprigs
orange, lemon and lime slices for garnish

Steep tea with cloves and cool. Combine juices with tea mixture and add ginger ale and rum. Serve in ice-filled glasses and garnish with mint and fruit slices.

SANDWICHES AND TIDBITS

TEA SANDWICH IDEAS

Tea sandwiches should look as good as they taste. Use your prettiest trays and platters and garnish with fresh herbs, flowers and fruit. For variety, make your own quick breads and freeze them weeks ahead. Consider using egg, whole wheat, black bread, rye or cheddar breads. Or try sweet breads such as banana, date nut, zucchini, orange or lemon. Breads should be thinly sliced and the crusts removed. Traditional circles, rolls, fingers, triangles and squares are quick to make. Consider using different cookie cutters to fit the occasion as well.

Spread slices with softened butter or mayonnaise. Leave some sandwiches open face. A certain uniformity and precision makes your presentation more special. Place sandwiches on cookie sheets and cover with a damp towel to keep them from drying out. Cover tightly with plastic wrap and store in the refrigerator.

Here are some ideas to get you started:

whole wheat bread, herbed cream cheese and English cucumbers

Brie cheese, ham and green peppercorn mustard on black bread

rye bread, unsalted butter, avocado, sliced hard cooked egg and a dollop of black caviar

mozzarella cheese, sliced plum tomato and a sprig of fresh basil on tiny baguettes radish butter on whole wheat garnished with watercress

dilled cream cheese, thinly sliced cucumber and baby shrimp on white bread

smoked salmon, cream cheese and sliced scallion on wheat bread

mascarpone cheese on black bread

ground ham, green peppercorns, Dijon mustard and mayonnaise on cheddar bread

cream cheese, chutney, curry and toasted almonds on banana bread

deviled egg and chives on egg bread

smoked turkey, mayonnaise and roasted red pepper on rye bread

pineapple cream cheese on mango bread

WATERCRESS TEA SANDWICHES

The ultimate in tea sandwiches, these were featured at the Savoy Hotel in London at their afternoon tea.

$1/2$ cup butter, softened
$1/2$ cup finely chopped watercress sprigs
2 tsp. grated onion
$3/4$ tsp. Worcestershire sauce
$1/4$ tsp. salt
$1/4$ tsp. white pepper
watercress sprigs for garnish
1 loaf (16 oz.) thinly sliced white bread

Combine butter, watercress sprigs and seasonings. Roll bread slices flat with a rolling pin and spread with butter mixture. Roll up. Cover with a damp paper towel, which has been wrung out tightly, and wrap well with plastic wrap. Refrigerate for up to 24 hours. Before serving, bring to room temperature, cut each sandwich in half and insert sprigs of watercress into each end.

JOANNA'S DATE BREAD

Makes 1 loaf

Moist and delicious, this is so good spread with pineapple cream cheese. It's nice to garnish these with a tiny wedge of fresh strawberry and a sprig of mint.

¼ cup butter
2 cups boiling water
1 pound pitted dates
2 tsp. baking soda
2 cups sugar
3½ cups flour
1 cup coarsely chopped walnuts

Bring water to a boil in a saucepan. Add butter and dates and let cool. When cool, add remaining ingredients in order listed. Heat oven to 325°. Grease a bread pan and line the bottom with a piece of parchment or brown paper. Pour batter into pan and bake for 1 hour or until loaf tests done. Wrap well and refrigerate or freeze.

MANGO BREAD

If fresh mangoes are not available, use frozen mango juice concentrate or canned mangoes, well drained. This is excellent spread with pineapple cream cheese.

¾ cup oil
2 eggs
1¼ cups sugar
2 cups flour
2 tsp. soda
2 tsp. cinnamon

½ tsp. salt
1 tsp. lemon juice
2½ cups chopped mangoes
1 cup raisins
1 cup coarsely chopped walnuts

In an electric mixer, combine oil, egg and sugar. Sift together flour, soda, cinnamon and salt. Add to egg mixture. Stir in lemon juice, mangoes, raisins and nuts. Pour into 2 greased 8 x 4-inch bread pans.

Heat oven to 350°. Bake for 1 hour, or until center of loaves test done. Cool. Wrap in foil and refrigerate or freeze.

STRAWBERRY TEA BREAD

This moist bread is delicious spread with strawberry or honey butter.

2 cups sugar
4 eggs
1¼ cups melted butter
2 pkg. (10 oz. each) frozen strawberries, including juice, thawed
3 cups flour
1 tsp. baking powder
1 tsp. salt
3 tsp. cinnamon
1¼ cups chopped pecans

Heat oven to 350°. Grease and flour 2 bread pans. Using an electric mixer, beat sugar, eggs and melted butter. Add strawberries and juice. Sift together flour, baking powder, salt and cinnamon. Add to strawberry mixture. Stir in pecans. Pour batter into pans. Bake for 1 hour. Cool for 10 minutes in the pan and turn out onto wire racks.

COCONUT REFRIGERATOR COOKIES

Makes 3 dozen

This recipe makes a lovely and delicate cookie to serve with tea. If you wish, you can dust the tops with powdered sugar or dip one half into melted dark chocolate.

1 cup butter, softened
1/4 cup sugar
1 tsp. vanilla extract
2 cups flour
1/4 tsp. salt
2 cups angel flake coconut

Cream together butter, sugar and vanilla using an electric mixer or food processor. Add flour, salt and coconut. It may be necessary to knead the coconut by hand in order to get it all mixed in. Divide dough in half. Shape into rolls, two inches in diameter. Wrap in plastic wrap. Refrigerate for 2 hours, or up to 3 days.

Heat oven to 300°. Slice rolls 1/4-inch thick using a sharp knife. Place on ungreased cookie sheet and bake for 20 minutes, until light golden brown. Cool on wire rack. Store cooled cookies in an airtight container.

CREAM SCONES

For best results, make sure your baking powder is fresh.

1³/₄ cup flour
2 tsp. baking powder
1 tbs. sugar
¹/₂ tsp. salt

¹/₄ cup butter
2 eggs, beaten
¹/₃ cup cream
1 tbs. sugar

Sift flour, baking powder, sugar and salt into a bowl. Cut butter into flour mixture using a pastry blender. Mixture should look like small peas. In another bowl, beat eggs and reserve 2 tbs. for glaze. Beat all but 2 tbs. of the eggs with cream. Add to flour mixture using swift strokes.

Divide dough in half. Pat each half out on a lightly floured board forming a circle ³/₄-inch thick, which is higher in the center. Cut each piece into 6 pie-shaped wedges. Place on a greased baking sheet with the thicker points facing the center of the sheet. Brush with the reserved beaten egg and sprinkle with the sugar.

Bake at 450° for 15 minutes, or until light gold. Serve hot with an assortment of jams.

SESAME CHEESE STRAWS

There are cheese straws and there are cheese straws - these are THE BEST!

2 cups flour
$2/3$ cup butter
2 cups shredded sharp cheddar cheese
$1/2$ cup toasted sesame seeds
1 tsp. salt
1 tsp. ground ginger
1 tsp. Worcestershire sauce
4 to 5 tbs. cold water

Heat oven to 400°. In a food processor using the steel blade, combine flour and butter. Add cheese, seeds and seasonings until mixture resembles coarse crumbs. Sprinkle with cold water and process until mixture begins to form a ball. Remove dough from the machine and roll out as for pie crust on a lightly floured board. Cut into decorative strips using a pastry cutter or sharp knife. Place on a lightly greased baking sheet and bake for 10 to 12 minutes, or until golden. Cool on a wire rack. Store in airtight containers. These freeze well.

SALMON-STUFFED CHERRY TOMATOES

Makes 3 dozen

These cheery little morsels always disappear from a tea tray in a hurry. This mixture is also good piped onto English cucumber rounds.

3 dozen cherry tomatoes
8 oz. cream cheese, softened
4 oz. butter, softened

4 oz. smoked salmon, chopped
4 green onions, sliced
sprigs of parsley

Hollow out cherry tomatoes using a grapefruit spoon. Turn upside down to drain on paper towels.

Using the steel knife of a food processor or an electric mixer, combine cream cheese and butter until light. Stir in remaining ingredients. Spoon or pipe into cherry tomatoes, garnish with a small leaf of parsley and refrigerate until serving.

VARIATIONS

Fill tomatoes with guacamole.

Use baby shrimp, crab meat or crumbled bacon instead of smoked salmon.

GOOD WITH TEA: MUFFINS, COOKIES, TARTS AND PUDDINGS

ORANGE MUFFINS

These muffins have a delicious citrus flavor that is a perfect accompaniment to a refreshing cup of tea.

½ cup orange juice
¼ cup vegetable oil
1 cup butter
1 cup sugar
4 eggs, separated

½ cup orange marmalade
2 tsp. grated orange zest
2½ cups flour
2 tsp. baking powder
1 tsp. salt

Heat oven to 375°. Grease 24 two-inch muffin cups. Combine orange juice and oil in a 1-cup glass measure. Beat butter with sugar and egg yolks until light and fluffy. Add marmalade and orange zest. Sift together flour, baking powder and salt. Add alternately to butter-egg mixture with orange juice and oil.

In a separate bowl, beat egg whites until stiff. Fold into batter. Spoon evenly into prepared muffin cups. Bake for 20 minutes, or until golden.

APRICOT BARS

These are a snap to make and taste great.

1 cup butter
1 cup sugar
1 egg yolk
2 cups flour
¾ cup walnuts
1 jar (10 oz.) apricot jam

Heat oven to 350°. Grease a 9 x 13-inch baking pan. In a food processor using the steel blade, combine butter, sugar, egg, flour and nuts until crumbly. Pat half of the mixture onto the bottom of prepared pan. Spread with jam and crumble remaining dough on top. Bake for 40 to 45 minutes. Cool and cut into bars.

MARMALADE COOKIES

Makes 3 dozen

These cookies are perfect with a cup of Constant Comment tea.

½ cup butter
1 cup sugar
2 eggs, beaten
3 cups flour

½ tsp. soda
½ tsp. salt
1 cup orange marmalade

Using an electric mixer, cream butter, sugar and eggs until light. Add flour, soda and salt. Stir in marmalade. Drop by rounded teaspoons 1 inch apart on greased cookie sheets. Bake at 350° for 10 to 12 minutes. Cool on wire racks.

FROSTING

¼ cup orange juice

2 tsp. orange zest
1 tsp. lemon juice

1 tsp. lemon zest
3 tbs. butter
3 cups powdered sugar

Combine frosting ingredients in a food processor using the steel knife. Frost cooled cookies.

BUTTER PECAN BARS

Makes 2 dozen

This decadent recipe is like blond brownies with pecan pie filling on top.

¾ cup butter
1½ cups brown sugar
2 eggs

2 tsp. vanilla extract
1¾ cups flour
1 tsp. soda

Using the steel knife of a food processor or an electric mixer, mix butter, sugar, egg and vanilla until creamy. Add flour and soda. Heat oven to 350°. Grease and flour a 9 x 13-inch pan. Spread batter in pan, smoothing evenly. Bake for 15 minutes.

TOPPING

½ cup butter
½ cup honey
½ cup brown sugar

1 tsp. instant coffee
3 tbs. cream
3 cups pecans, chopped

In a heavy saucepan, melt butter. Stir in honey, brown sugar, coffee and cream. Over medium heat, bring to a boil stirring constantly. Remove from heat. Add pecans and pour onto prepared crust. Bake at 350° for 25 minutes. Cool and cut into bars.

HONEY NUT CHEWS

To decorate, drizzle thin lines of melted white and dark chocolate across the top.

CRUST

²/₃ cups powdered sugar

2 cups flour

1 cup butter

Heat oven to 350°. Grease and flour a 9 x 13-inch baking pan. Using the steel blade of a food processor, or an electric mixer, combine crust ingredients until crumbly and pat into prepared pan. Bake for 20 minutes and cool.

TOPPING

1 cup slivered almonds

1 cup coarsely chopped walnuts

1 cup coarsely chopped pecans

½ cup butter, melted

½ cup honey

½ cup brown sugar

Prepare nuts by rinsing them in a strainer. Spread on a cookie sheet and bake at 350° for 5 to 10 minutes, until completely dry and lightly toasted. In a large bowl, stir together melted butter, honey and brown sugar. Add toasted nuts and stir to coat well. Spread carefully over prepared crust and bake at 350° for 20 to 25 minutes. Cool and drizzle with melted chocolate, if desired. Cut into bars.

PECAN TASSIES

Teflon-lined miniature muffin tins are also good for appetizers and desserts.

CRUST

1 cup butter

6 oz. cream cheese

2 cups flour

Heat oven to 350°. Using the steel blade of a food processor, combine butter, cream cheese and flour until it forms a smooth dough. Remove from workbowl and divide evenly into fourths. Divide each portion into 12 small balls. Spray 4 miniature muffin pans (12 muffins each) with non-stick coating. Press each ball of dough into a muffin cup evenly on bottom and up sides to rim.

FILLING

1/2 cup butter, softened

2 eggs, beaten

1 cup sugar

1 1/2 cup pecans, chopped

1 cup dates, pitted and chopped

2 tsp. vanilla extract

Cream together butter and eggs. Stir in remaining ingredients. Divide evenly among unbaked shells. Fill completely. Bake until golden brown, about 30 to 40 minutes. Cool before removing from tins. If desired, sprinkle with powdered sugar before serving.

RASPBERRY KUCHEN

Makes 16–20 wedges

This is a buttery rich Dutch cookie, perfect to serve with tea. Its success depends on using a quality jam—we like raspberry or apricot. And NEVER use anything but real butter!!

2²/₃ cups flour
1¹/₃ cups sugar
1¹/₃ cups butter
¹/₂ tsp. salt
1 egg
2 cups jam, raspberry or apricot

Using the steel blade of a food processor, combine flour, sugar, butter and salt until crumbly. Press ²/₃ of the dough into the bottom of a buttered 9-inch springform pan. Spread with jam. Crumble remaining dough on top. Bake at 350° for 45 minutes, or until golden. Cool and cut into small wedges to serve.

AMARETTO BREAD PUDDING

Try this with a cup of apricot tea. A bain marie *is a French water bath: set baking dish into a larger pan and pour boiling water half way up the side of the dish.*

1½ lb. egg bread, torn into pieces
4½ cups milk
1½ cups cream
5 eggs, beaten
2¼ cups sugar

3 tbs. almond extract
1 cup dried apricots, chopped
2 cups golden raisins
1¼ cups slivered almonds

Pour milk and cream over bread and let stand for 10 minutes. Combine remaining ingredients and mix well with softened bread. Pour into a well-buttered baking dish and bake at 350° for 50 to 60 minutes in a hot water bath (*bain marie*).

AMARETTO SAUCE

1 cup butter
2 cups powdered sugar, sifted

2 eggs, beaten
½ cup amaretto

Melt butter in a saucepan over low heat. Stir in powdered sugar and eggs, whisking constantly. Add amaretto to taste. Pour hot sauce over individual servings of the bread pudding.

RAISIN BREAD PUDDING

Servings: 10–12

This is comfort food at its best. Add a cup of hot tea and you're all set!

1 loaf (16 oz.) cinnamon raisin bread
1 qt. milk
3 eggs

2 cups sugar
2 tbs. vanilla extract
1 tbs. butter

Tear bread into large pieces and place in a large mixing bowl. Pour milk over and stir to coat. Let bread soak for 15 minutes.

Beat eggs, sugar and vanilla until thick and smooth. Pour over bread mixture and combine well. Place in a well-buttered baking dish. Heat oven to 350°. Place pudding in a larger pan and fill with 2 inches of hot water. Bake for 1 hour, or until set. If desired, serve with *Whiskey Sauce.*

WHISKEY SAUCE

1 cup heavy cream
4 egg yolks

1 cup powdered sugar
¼ cup whiskey

Beat cream until stiff. Beat egg yolks in a separate bowl; add powdered sugar and whip until light. Add whiskey and fold in whipped cream.

INDEX

Serve Creative, Easy, Nutritious Meals with nitty gritty® Cookbooks

100 Dynamite Desserts
The 9 x 13 Pan Cookbook
The Barbecue Cookbook
Beer and Good Food
Best Bagels are Made at Home
Best Pizza is Made at Home
Big Book of Bread Machine Recipes
Big Book of Kitchen Appliance Recipes
Big Book of Snacks & Appetizers
Blender Drinks
Bread Baking
Bread Machine Cookbook
Bread Machine Cookbook II
Bread Machine Cookbook III
Bread Machine Cookbook V
Bread Machine Cookbook VI
The Little Burger Bible
Cappuccino/Espresso
Casseroles
The Coffee and Tea Cookbook
Convection Oven Cookery
The Cook-Ahead Cookbook
Cooking for 1 or 2

Cooking in Clay
Cooking on the Indoor Grill
Cooking in Porcelain
Cooking with Chile Peppers
Cooking with Grains
Cooking with Your Kids
New Recipes for your Deep Fryer
The Dehydrator Cookbook
Edible Pockets for Every Meal
Entrees from Your Bread Machine
Extra-Special Crockery Pot Recipes
Fabulous Fiber Cookery
Fondue and Hot Dips
Fresh Vegetables
From Freezer, 'Fridge and Pantry
The Garlic Cookbook
Healthy Cooking on the Run
Healthy Snacks for Kids
From Your Ice Cream Maker
The Juicer Book
The Juicer Book II
Lowfat American Favorites
New International Fondue Cookbook

No Salt, No Sugar, No Fat
One-Dish Meals
The Pasta Machine Cookbook
Pinch of Time: Meals in Less than 30
   Minutes
Quick and Easy Low-Carb Recipes
Quick and Easy Pasta Recipes
Quick and Easy Soy and Tofu Recipes
Recipes for the Loaf Pan
Recipes for the Pressure Cooker
Rotisserie Oven Cooking
New Recipes for Your Sandwich Maker
The Sensational Skillet: Sautés and Stir-Fries
Slow Cooking in Crock-Pot,® Slow Cooker,
   Oven and Multi-Cooker
Simple Substitutions Cookbook
Soups and Stews
Tapas Fantasticas
The Toaster Oven Cookbook
Unbeatable Chicken Recipes
The Vegetarian Slow Cooker
New Waffles and Pizzelles
Wraps and Roll-Ups

For a free catalog, call: Bristol Publishing Enterprises.
(800) 346-4889
www.bristolpublishing.com